CBI Headquarters

Victory or Mystery?

Attention Authors

'We Convert Fighters into Writers'. That's the motto of Manas Publications since more than four decades. Our message to the world is that India can win the battle not only by the bullet but also by the pen. There is no dearth of intellectuals in our country, but their knowledge is confined to them only. No sincere effort has been made by any other publisher to channelise their knowledge in national interest. That is why the talent of a large number of intellectuals remains latent. An author transforms his knowledge into a manuscript, and it is the publisher's job to spread his/her knowledge by converting it into a beautiful book. For over four decades, Manas has been motivating the intellectuals by publishing their manuscripts and would like to publish your manuscript too. If you or your colleagues have any manuscript ready for publication or are working on it, kindly contact us with detailed synopsis and list of contents. We will transform your work into a valuable publication. If you wish, we can also suggest you the suitable subjects for writing the books related to your area of expertise. Manas is known for its publishing quality and commitments. We take utmost care in production and give wide publicity to the book as well as its author through our national and international distribution network.

CBI Headquarters

Victory or Mystery?

D Mukherjee, IPS

Former: Addl Director, CBI
DGP Tamil Nadu

Manas Publications
(We Convert Fighters into Writers)
New Delhi-110002 (INDIA)

MANAS PUBLICATIONS

(We Convert Fighters into Writers)

(Publishers, Library Suppliers, Importers & Exporters)
4402/5-A, Ansari Road (Opp HDFC Bank)
Darya Ganj, New Delhi-110 002 (India)
Off. ✆ 23260783, 23265523, Fax: 011-23272766
E-mail: manaspublications@vsnl.com
manaspublications@gmail.com

ISBN 978-81-7049-447-8
₹ 595/-

Designed at
Manas Publications

Printed in India at
HS Offsets, Delhi
and published by Mrs Suman Lata for
Manas Publications, 4402/5-A,
Ansari Road (Opp HDFC Bank),
Darya Ganj, New Delhi-110 002 (INDIA)

CONTENTS

PREFACE

Although I joined the Police Service driven by a resolve, the meaningless regimentation and bullying by some superiors led to bouts of depression and there were moments when I seriously contemplated quitting and going back to my academic world. Cajoled by some well-wishers, I stuck on. However, I realised that there was a silver lining too. Soon it dawned on me that there was a lighter vein and no dearth of humorous moments, thanks to an overzealous constabulary.

I started collecting these anecdotes at every place of posting with the idea of compiling the same in a book form. Somehow this desire got integrated with my memoirs. In fact, in the narration of my initial career I tried to highlight the lighter side of life, but slowly serious matters started creeping in which makes the book an admixture of light as well as serious matters.

Since I have spent more than one third of my service life in CBI, the organisation has received more coverage. Perhaps it is justified also in view of its importance today.

In training we are taught "know your men" to have a grip on the administration. I took this advice seriously and freely interacted with my staff irrespective of the rank. From all of them I could get valuable inputs about legends, traditions, profiles of interesting characters of the force and enchanting stories about their idiosyncrasies. This information has contributed substantially towards this humble presentation which is based broadly on my own experience.

Introduction

When I was asked to execute the non-bailable warrants issued by a Delhi Court against the godman Chandraswamy and his aide Kailash Nath Agarwal alias 'Mamaji' I took it as a routine police job and did not expect the extent of sensation it created and the coverage it got in the media. More surprising was the interest generated amongst retired officers and their eagerness to hear the details of the operation. The association of retired IPS Officers (FORMPOL) extended an invitation to me to attend their next bi-monthly meeting as their guest. The former Generals requested me to narrate my experience with the controversial godman.

After I had finished recounting the course of events with minute details, Mr KR Shenai, former Director General of Police commented, "Mukherjee, you must write a book". Acting on his advice, I quickly wrote down the sequence of events of that fateful night, but realised that this alone would not be sufficient to constitute a book and resolved to start from the beginning and cover the entire period of my career in the Indian Police Service incorporating, *inter-alia*, the Chandraswamy episode.

Narration of most of the incidents concerning my batchmates is based on personal memory and not any documents. Some of the anecdotes are collected from other colleagues - senior as well as contemporary officers. If anyone does not agree I beg his forgiveness and submit that these should be taken in a lighter vein and the episodes viewed for their humour content alone if not for their authenticity.

As far as the narration of the cases is concerned I have tried to confine myself to the findings of the courts, but highlighted the salient features of the investigation, especially the stumbling blocks. It has not been possible to include all cases dealt by me, but only those of topical interest.

I have drawn inspiration from many officers for a meaningful pursuit of my career in police service. It has not been possible to mention all of them individually, since those personally involved with the episodes described only were selected for exclusive mention. That does not lower my respect and regards for anyone of them. I salute all of them.

It was my mother, who brought me up against all odds and facilitated my entry into the bureaucratic world. I dedicate this humble effort to her departed soul. I owe a big thanks to my wife, who helped me with tireless secretarial assistance apart from serving as a constant source of encouragement.

Chapter – 1

Arrest of Godman Chandraswamy
A Night to Remember

A landmark event whose minute to minute development will remain ingrained in my memory was the arrest of the renowned spiritual leader godman Chandraswamy. Theoretically, it was rather a simple matter. It was a central unit case (Lakhubhai Pathak case) which was already pending trial in a Delhi Court. The Chief Metropolitan Magistrate, Delhi had issued a non-bailable warrant after court taking cognizance of the warrant case and our job was restricted to executing the same. Practically, however, the task was not so simple in view of the personality involved. Further, the operation required perfect coordination with other agencies and planning at every step. In fact, it turned out to be a mammoth exercise in organizing ability.

It was election day in Madras and happened to be a holiday. Around 7 pm on 2nd May 1996 when I was about to leave for visiting a friend I got a call from RC Sharma, Additional Director, later became the Director, CBI, intimating that a warrant was issued and the same had to be executed at Madras since Chandraswamy was camping there. Immediately, I got in touch with SSB, CID and ascertained that the godman was staying in Sindoori

Hotel , adjoining Apollo Hospital. Since the execution of the warrant was to take some more time, I requested SSB to mount surveillance on the hotel to monitor his movements.

I tried to muster manpower and vehicles by contacting SP CBI. She was not readily available. Three days being holidays many of the staff were availing the same. Fifteen minutes later, Anand Kumar Joint Director came on the line and informed that he will be sending the warrant by fax. I asked him to send the same on my personal number at Shastri Bhavan, Madras (now Chennai). By contacting the night duty constable, I learnt that the key of the room where the fax machine was installed was not available. I asked him to break open the lock and retrieve the warrant.

I was able to contact PM Goud, SP, SCB. Since he had a transport, I requested him to pick me up and also bring along any available DySP or Inspector. Simultaneously, I left a message with the sentry at KK Nagar, CBI quarters to despatch any DySP or Inspector available to Sindoori Hotel. As I was waiting for Mr Goud to pick me up, Mr Bhoopathy Babu, SP Special Unit conveyed the instructions of the Director to report the developments. He promised to come to the hotel with the available staff. Soon Mrs Srilakshmi Prasad, SP also contacted me and I asked her to come to the hotel along with any law officer available.

Mr Goud arrived with DySP Mr Pandiarajan around 8 pm and we dashed off to the Sindoori Hotel.

On arrival, I found Mrs Srilakshmi Prasad and Inspector Nazer already present. There were some gun-totting commandos and three or four security vehicles near the portico. I was under the impression that these people had come for Chandraswamy. I told Mrs Prasad to wait at the hotel along with Mr Goud SP, DySP and the Inspector till I returned with the warrant from Shastri Bhavan. Mrs Prasad enquired what she was supposed to do if Chandraswamy attempted to escape. I asked her to apprehend him in that case.

On reaching Shastri Bhavan which was just three minutes drive, I found that the duty staff had already broken open the door and retrieved the fax message. Realising that there may be attempts to resist arrest, I asked the armed sentry to accompany me to face any eventuality. Necessary entries were made in the sentry relief book and an unarmed PC was deployed to guard the office.

When I returned to the Sindoori Hotel , I was surprised to see that the commandos and their vehicles had vanished. For a moment, I felt my heart stopping at the premonition that the godman had escaped. None of my team members was to be seen at the portico. With a feeling of void I was simply gazing at the sky. My driver was more spirited and went around reccing the place. He quickly discovered that our team members already informed by the Press Information Bureau, Delhi about the issuance of non-bailable warrants against Chandraswamy and others were available at the lobby. I rushed in, only to land in a crowd of newsmen and people from various TV channels with their bulky cameras. They surrounded me and started their volleys of questions. They were already informed by the Press Information Bureau, Delhi about the issuance of non-bailable warrants against Chandraswamy and his associate KN Agarwal *alias* Mamaji. I requested the Pressmen to wait till our operation was over.

I sat in the lobby and endorsed the warrant to the SP for execution. She in turn endorsed it to Inspector Nazer. Both of them went upstairs to the first floor where Chandraswamy was occupying a suite. Incidentally, the commandos, that I had seen earlier were learnt to be on duty with Dr Subramaniyaswamy, who had visited the place earlier. After about fifteen minutes, the SP came back to the lobby and whispered that there was some problem. Requesting the Pressmen to stay back I went to the first floor. The two warrantees were occupying a corner suite. Two-three neighbouring rooms were occupied by the bodyguards. They were stout people with shaven heads. Perhaps this was linked to their visit to Tirupati.

The godman Chandraswamy was lying on the bed. KN Agarwal was sitting on one side of the bed with a telephone and frantically trying some number. Apparently, the SP had tried and failed to convey the crux of the matter to Chandraswamy. The latter was pretending as if he did not understand English. He looked at me with bulging eyes and queried in Hindi, "Will someone explain as to what is going on here"? I replied (in Hindi) that the CMM, Delhi had issued a warrant and I had to execute the same. He appeared very disturbed and argued, "I have already obtained bail in this case". I said, "I have to carry out the orders of the court". Chandraswamy again argued that he was not well and not in a position to move as he was having severe pain in the neck. I offered medical help before removing him from the hotel.

By this time, Agarwal had returned to the anteroom to try the telephone unhindered. The SP informed me that he was not willing to disclose his identity. I intervened and asked his name. He did not respond. I asked whether he was Mamaji. He kept mum. I tried again, "Are you Mamaji? What is your name"? At this he responded, "I will tell you later". By this point of time, I had reached the end of my patience and made a final bid, "What is the problem in disclosing your name"? It seems that earlier he had given a comical reply to the SP, "We belong to the spiritual world. Now, I am moving in that world and can disclose my name only after coming back". At this juncture, he was told that the warrant included his name and he was being arrested. He just slumped into the bed with hands on his chest as if he had a heart problem.

At this point of time, the media had come up to the first floor and started crowding the area. To keep them at bay, I came out and requested them to come with me to the lobby. They readily agreed and came down along with me. Seeing the delay, they had become suspicious about the genuineness of the CBI operation and unanimously shot the same question, "Are you really going to arrest Chandraswamy"? I informed them that the arrest had already been effected.

There was some delay in the procedure. But they were not satisfied and went on to enquire whether I was under any pressure from the PMO. I stoutly denied the baseless insinuation. In the meantime, there was a message from Director CBI requiring me to speak to him. I went to the room of the hotel manager from where I could contact Vijay Rama Rao, Director CBI. After ascertaining the situation he instructed me—

To ensure that there was no harassment or ill-treatment to anybody, and to brief the press properly.

Again I returned to Chandraswamy. In the meantime, Dr Subramaniyaswamy along with Smt TMT Chandralekha came back and demanded to know the course of action proposed by us. He was informed by the SP that Chandraswamy has been arrested and being remanded. At this Dr Subramaniyaswamy pointed out that he was already on bail and could not be arrested. He also called G Ramaswamy, former Attorney General on his cell phone and briefed him about the CBI action. He suggested that I should speak to the former AG. My officers pleaded that we should not get entangled in arguments with such an eminent lawyer. I knew what Mr Ramaswamy was going to say and told my officers that there was no harm in talking. Dr Subramaniyaswamy handed over the phone to me. As expected, Mr Ramaswamy started, "I do not want to interfere in your duty, I just wanted to know the case details and the section of law". On providing the requisite information he remarked, "I have already obtained bail in this case". I said, "I do not know about that but I have received a lawful order and I have to carry it out". Mr Ramaswamy enquired, "Are you going to produce him before the magistrate tonight itself"? I replied in the affirmative. At this point of time, he wanted to know if we could give half an hour time, so that some advocate may be made available. I readily agreed.

It was again pointed out that Chandraswamy was sick and was being taken in custody against medical advice. I agreed to doctors being brought for treatment of

Chandraswamy before moving to the court. Promptly, two doctors arrived from Apollo Hospital (the next building). They left after thorough check up of Chandraswamy.

In the meantime, sensing some possible resistance, I had telephoned to Mr G Veeraraghavan, IPS COP, Chennai and requested deployment of local police for security. Inspector, Thousand Lights police station turned up immediately with his team although they had a very tiring election day. Two advocates deputed by Mr G Ramaswamy also arrived at the scene.

They brought law books along with them and started arguing on the point that warrant could not be issued in a case where bail has already been granted. I simply requested them to reserve the arguments till the production of the warrantees before the court.

In the meanwhile, another drama was going on regarding the availability of magistrate for granting transit remand. Mr R Soundararajan, Public Prosecutor, CBI, who was available on the spot with us contacted the CMM and requested him to come over to Sindoori Hotel for granting remand. The Public Prosecutor was asked to meet him with the requisite application. However, by the time, the PP could meet him the latter had changed his mind and put an endorsement on the application to the effect. "Since the arrested person is not produced before me I am not in a position to give transit remand". This further complicated the matter and prolonged the sequence of events. When Mr Soundararajan returned empty handed, we held a discussion and it was decided to approach the incharge Principal Sessions Judge for CBI cases, Mr Sambandham. On being contacted over telephone by the PP, he agreed to grant the remand and asked the accused to be produced before him at his residence.

In the meantime, I had made arrangements for both a stretcher as well as a wheel chair for transporting Chandraswamy in view of his complaint of illness. He preferred the wheelchair. When the chair was brought into his room some of his aides kept on abusing us alleging illtreatment. Chandraswamy himself was only worried about the possé of Pressmen and wanted an assurance that they will not cover the event. Although Mr Goud SP gave the assurance, we knew how difficult it was to clear the hotel lobby of all the Pressmen and photographers. As Chandraswamy sat in the wheelchair, his friends and aides showed signs of resistance. At this point, I asked the Inspector of Thousand Lights police station to arrest anyone trying to obstruct us in the discharge of our duties. There was no further problem and our people started slowly rolling out Chandraswamy into the corridor towards the lift. I came out of the room to clear the corridor and requested all the Pressmen to wait in the lobby. At the portico, an ambulance provided by the Apollo Hospital was kept ready, but the godman was requested to travel in the CBI vehicle and accordingly the convoy was arranged. I gave instructions to the driver to move very slowly, as Chandraswamy had complained of neck pain.

As the wheelchair carrying Chandraswamy rolled out of the lift, cameras started flashing which enraged the godman and he found fault with the SP, "You have cheated me, you promised there would be no Press". However, soon he realised the futility of protesting further and quietly got into the car.

The vehicle carrying Chandraswamy and Mamaji was followed by a convoy carrying myself, Bhupati Babu, PM Goud and Srilakshmi Prasad along with Public Prosecutor Soundararajan. The Press people and TV cameramen followed us in their vehicles and the carcade comprised of more than twenty vehicles. We started around 1.30 am and after a long journey we reached the residence of A Sambandham, Additional Special Judge at Saligramam. The accused were taken inside and on my request the Pressmen agreed to wait outside. The judge convened the court at his residence. On behalf of the accused, advocate Kumar appeared and Soundararajan, Public Prosecutor represented the CBI. During the course of arguments, the judge was informed that Chandraswamy was ill and undergoing treatment at the Apollo Hospital. The judge immediately rang up the hospital to confirm the fact and received a reply in the negative. At this Chandraswamy demanded the fact to be verified from a doctor, he mentioned specifically. The judge telephoned the doctor. The latter's wife took the phone but the doctor refused to come on line. At this point, the judge remarked that in that case, he had no other option but to grant transit remand. However, he agreed to allow a medical officer to accompany Chandraswamy upto Delhi. The counsel for Chandraswamy demanded that CBI meet the expenditure to be incurred. I readily agreed to include the expenditure in our account.

While the arguments were going on, anticipating the grant of transit remand, I took a decision to take the accused straight to the airport and put them on the morning flight as it was already 3 am and there was hardly any point in going back to CBI office and keeping them in our custody for a longer period, which was fraught with risk. It was not prudent to allow crowds to congregate. Even before the judge started writing his order, I despatched one team headed by Mr Ramaswamy, DySP in advance to the airport for booking tickets in respect of Chandraswamy, Mamaji, two members of the CBI escort team and one doctor. In another vehicle, I sent SP PM Goud and Inspector Nazer, who executed the warrant, to go home and collect their dress for going to Delhi as escort and report at the airport. I detailed another party to escort Chandraswamy and Mamaji to the airport with instructions to put them in the lounge. After seeing off the various parties, I returned to Shastri Bhahvan to collect air vouchers for purchase of tickets. There was only one constable Chandrasekharan available in the office. After a lot of rummaging, he could locate the voucher book and I secured the required blank vouchers. Before leaving for the airport, I rang up Anand Kumar, Joint Directror of CBI, Delhi who was incharge of this case and informed him about the completion of the task assigned and my decision to put the accused on the morning flight. I also requested him to make necessary arrangements at Delhi airport. He thanked me profoundly and remarked that the image of CBI was saved.

By the time, I reached the airport it was around 5 am. Air vouchers were presented and tickets purchased quickly. I could see the godman's bodyguards and other aides with travel bags roaming around and ready to take the flight. The private secretary of the owner of Apollo Hospital was personally present to make the arrangements. Srilakshmi Prasad SP reported that the defence had informed that their doctor was not prepared to accompany. She also informed me that Chandraswamy had complained of chest pain. Promptly, the duty medical officer of the Airport Authority of India was summoned. She took ECG picture of Chandraswamy and checked his BP and found no abnormality. However, she told our staff that since Chandraswamy had mentioned about his previous heart ailment, taking him to Delhi was at our own risk.

Since the judicial order stipulated a medical officer to accompany and as a doctor nominated by the accused refused to accompany, we requested the Indian Airlines in writing to depute their doctor to proceed to Delhi in the same flight. The Indian Airlines regretted their inability to comply with our request. We took these steps to guard against any allegation of contempt of court. When our officers were feeling nervous on the observations of the duty doctor, I convinced them –"Chandraswamy has complained of an ailment and on checking by a medical officer, the ECG and BP are found to be normal and no treatment was considered necessary. We have asked the doctor to treat his ailment and not issue a fitness certificate. In any case, we expect some doctor to be on board amongst the passengers to take care of any emergency". At that point of time, the door of the VIP lounge opened a bit and we could see Chandraswamy doing *yoga* in the lounge. Soon departure was announced and I sat in a chair outside the lounge. Some journalists were seen loitering around. They appreciated CBI's action and congratulated me and my team.

As Chandraswamy was rolled out of the lounge, an airport authority security guard came up and enquired whether hand-cuffs were required. We smilingly declined. Chandraswamy was taken in the lift and then upto the aircraft through the aerobridge. I waited on the aerobridge till the door closed and the aircraft started taking off. I left the airport only after the flight took off. By the time, I reached home it was 7.15 am. I rang up Vijay Rama Rao, Director CBI and reported compliance of the task given to me. He thanked me profusely for having handled the matter tactfully and despatching the accused to Delhi with utmost speed. I could not keep my eyes open any longer and slumped into my bed – only to be woken up repeatedly through congratulatory calls.

As requested by Anand Kumar, Joint Director, EOW I prepared a list of all CBI personnel, including me, who played some role or the other in the night-long operation and submitted a reward roll for approval of the Director. The same never saw the light of the day. On the other hand, when I attempted to check up the status of the matter from Anand Kumar, he remarked jocularly, "The warrant was sent to you, but you were not expected to act".

Chapter - 2

Entry in Indian Police Service

In my formative years, I never had any fancy for the bureaucracy. In fact, the arrogant demeanour of some of the specimens - I had chance to have a glimpse of–was enough to evoke a sense of contempt against the species in general. I had no inkling that one day I was going to be a part of the same institution, thanks to an unsavoury incident that provoked me to join the police.

That was my first year in college. One evening, I was late for home and pedalling down absent-mindedly, became a soft target for the Kotwali police, who were conducting their usual monthly drive to complete the quota of petty cases. Defaulters were made to dismount from their bicycles and herded into the police station. We were let off after noting down our names and addresses. The charge was "riding a cycle without light". Thank God, this legislation has become history in Tamil Nadu along with another infringement "doubles". These legislations were very much in force when I was an ASP.

I forgot about the matter. After three years, I was shocked to find a head constable from the local outpost knocking at our door with a bailable warrant. The Section of law infringed was 15 PMC (Patna Municipal Corporation) Act. The fact that my uncle was a deputy superintendent of police did not deter the head constable from accepting a courteous behaviour fee of Rs 2 from my father. The visit by the cop triggered off a high drama at home with no one in a position to identify the offence. Even a lawyer friend of my father could not throw any light till I appeared in the court to find out that it was a three years old petty case covered by the PMC Act. People at home took it for granted that the call from the court must have emanated from my participation in some student agitation. No amount of denial would convince them. As regards the mystery of the warrant, it seems, initially summons were issued and the local outpost returned the same, mischievously noting – 'addressee not available'. Naturally, the next step was a warrant.

On the stipulated date, I proceeded to the court accompanied by my father, an elder brother and the lawyer. In the Court Hall the Magistrate was going through the morning newspaper with nobody inside. It was a morning court and the Magistrate's clerk was standing outside. When my lawyer requested him to put up my case, he shouted that he had not yet finished his breakfast. The lawyer picked up the hint and took him to the canteen. Satisfied, the clerk immediately put up the case and on admission I was let off with a fine of five rupees as in the case of other persons.

I was so upset with the behaviour of the police that I decided to join the force myself with a view of setting things right from within. Thus, an adversary of the system became its part and my career dream veered a full 180 degrees from unravelling the mysteries of science to chasing criminals.

The anguish against the system emanated from a misdeed perpetrated by a functionary of the force in Bihar. Hence, the resolution to cleanse from within concerned that state only. To my misfortune, I missed a slot in my home state, but to my good luck I landed up in Tamil Nadu – a cadre well-known for its efficiency and good traditions.

Chapter - 3

First Ladder in Police

Tee-totaller does not fit

Come July and lo and behold the new batch has arrived. The campus at National Academy of Administration is bustling with activity. You can see them swarming the campus, the library point, Khulri Bazaar, Hari's canteen – in fact, all over Mussorie. The panorama of this lovely Hill Station would be incomplete without the flock of budding bureaucrats – the probationers. For many of them, especially those hailing from middle and lower middle classes it is a different world. The visits by the tailors, Jackson and Shobha to mention a few, for stitching the dinner jackets and blazers, the daily knock by the boy from Hari's canteen, sermons on table manners, the protocol at dinner nights and mess nights are all components of a totally new life style.

On a modest approximation, I found that about 30 per cent of the population had already experienced what they called, "one of the pleasures of life" – referring to the ecstasy provided by the bio-chemical effect of the wonder liquid -'alcohol'. Twenty-five years later at a dinner hosted by my chief, he was surprised to find me a teetotaller and remarked that I was missing the pleasures of life. On other occasions also I had to encounter similar references. At a party hosted by the Police Chief in Dubai, one Arab police officer quipped, "How is it! You are a police officer but don't drink"? Exactly the same words came out from a Union Minister, who had invited me to a dinner to discuss vigilance matters pertaining to his ministry. Till today I have not been able to appreciate as to how alcohol could be a pleasure of life or that a teetotaller does not fit in to the image of a police officer.

Nevertheless, a considerable majority of the teetotaller variety at the Academy believed that without personally experimenting, they could not confirm whether it was really a pleasure or not. So, they decided to ape the 30 per cent minority, who incidentally, came from affluent families. A few of the experimenters were quick to realise that pleasures brought in misery also, but a large section found it difficult to ward off the temptation and by the end of the foundation course, only less than 30 per cent remained unaffected.

My intention is not to launch a research into the pros and cons of the habit of drinking. On the other hand, it proved to be great entertainment to watch my colleagues smart under the effect of over-dosage. Within that short span of four months there were plenty of interesting incidents, which got ingrained in my memory for years to come. I treasure them very fondly. The same story was repeated at Mt Abu. While the vast majority of us were provided accommodation within the campus at Mussorie, others, especially those who joined late, had to settle for cottages outside. These had romantic names, such as Cosy Nook, Cosy Cot, Glenmire, Bright Lands etc. We had a separate mess for breakfast and dinner. For lunch, we had to join the majority at the Central Mess within the campus.

At Glenmire, I had to share a room with Venkat Ramani, Indian Revenue Service—an orthodox Tamil Brahmin. The other inmates in our area of the cottage were Ansar Ali, IRS—who met with a fatal accident a few years later, and RB Sreekumar, IPS—who hit the headlines by his bold report filed as intelligence chief of Gujarat with reference to the

Godhra riots. He was a jovial person and widely read. Often he would rake up ideological issues with Venkat Ramani and tease him. After having provoked Venkat to a point of no return he will suddenly get up to ease himself with a bang and take leave in the middle of the discussion, with Venkat fuming and fretting.

Sreekumar, who was a teetotaller, often used to join his friends for dinner in the Central Mess. Many of his friends had already been initiated while the remaining got baptized at Mussorie. My roommate did not want to be left behind. So, one evening, he joined the pre-dinner session at Ashok Bhavan and later accompanied his pals for dinner. Perhaps the dose was too much for a novice and he was already riding high. A probationer attempted to greet, "Hi Kumar!" My friend replied with bloody eyes, "How dare you call me Kumar? You should call me Kumar ji. Even Mohan used to call me Kumar ji". The friend was highly perplexed, "What are you talking Kumar? Who is Mohan"? Pat came the reply, "You don't know Mohan? Mohandas Karamchand Gandhi". Before people could react, Kumar got up from the table and rushed towards the washroom. He had to be carried to the room of a probationer nearby. Next morning only he returned to Glenmire–complaining of severe headache. Venkat, who seemed to relish every part of the incident, broke the story.

The rooms in the rear portion of our cottage were occupied by RK Majumdar, VK Joshi, Kamal Kumar and NK Mohanty, all IPS. One August night, we heard a commotion in their room. Sreekumar, Venkat and I rushed in along with Rahul Gopal from the nearby cottage. The scene was frightful. Majumdar with only his brief on was pacing up and down with a butcher's knife in his hand and repeatedly muttering, "there was no rain today, and even then my umbrella has been stolen" (umbrella lifting was very common at the Central Mess). He continued, "That Johny Sharma must have stolen my umbrella. I will kill him". When no cajoling would help, force had to be used to snatch the knife and put him in the bed. Soon he fell asleep and we returned to our quarters.

Then there was that rainy night. We had returned from dinner and were gossiping. Suddenly, there was a thud and we came out of the room. Someone had fallen down the slope and was trying to get up. Soon we recognised –it was PKB Chakravorty, IPS. He had ventured to drop in at Majumdar's place after dinner. Perhaps his dinner was as wet as the evening. While coming down the spiralling mud track leading to our cottage, he would have missed the track at the last bend and slid down, say ten feet. I and Sreekumar helped him get out of the slush. It was still raining heavily.

The most amusing of the incidents was a string of occurrences that took place on the Independence Day 1971. After the flag hoisting ceremony at the Academy, there was a spontaneous formation of a group incorporating probationers from all services which decided on a trek-cum-picnic with Kemptee falls as the venue. There were about fifteen of us. We assembled at the gate of the Academy. Lunch packs were lifted from the Central Mess and a few bottles of whiskey and beer purchased from Bhai Mohan Singh shop at the gate. These were to be opened at Kemptee falls. Some of the extra—brave ones, however, thought this was not enough and entered a Tibetan restaurant en route and gulped some *Chhang,* perhaps brewed from rice.

The trek to Kemptee took about an hour. There were several hairpin bends on the way. Near one such bend, a couple of adventurous persons, namely, Wangdi, IFS, and Aloke Majumdar, IRS, thought upon a brilliant idea of saving precious time by not following the hairpin bend, instead sliding down the slope to join the road below via a semi-vertical path. Perhaps the Tibetan brew had already started acting, keeping the foolishness behind such an attempt wide outside their mind frame. Before others could shout words of caution, the brave duo from West Bengal was sliding down the 60 feet slope. Luckily, both landed on their buttocks. We rushed down the hairpin bend. Their palms were badly bruised and gaping holes created on rear side of their trousers. There was no first aid kit around and we had to keep trudging along. Soon, we reached the falls and spread ourselves around at the base.

Maybe the heat generated by the drink was too much to bear for a few and they found comfort in the chill waters of the falls, with only underwear on. Aloke Majumdar, squatting below the water column, reminded us of Rajesh Khanna in *Kati Patang*. While most of the people spread out on the surrounding rocks, a few occupied the small shed adjoining the falls. I was one of them. We were having lunch here. Wangdi had already forgotten the nasty slip down the slope. Although he knew that I was Mukherjee, he kept on addressing me as Bhattacharya even after the error was pointed out by Bramha of Central Services. While munching his ham sandwich Wangdi queried –"Bhattacharya, you don't drink"? I said, "No". "That's great", he observed. A couple of minutes later he reverted back to the same topic. "Bhattacharya, sure you don't drink"? Time and again, he would repeat the same question and mutter "great *yaar*! "that's great" etc–every time I replied in the negative.

Around 3.30 pm we wound up and started our climb back. When most of us reached the main road, a small group was still climbing up from the base of the falls. Prashanto Roy, IRS, was one of them. Not finding him around, his friend Aloke Majumdar started crying like a child, "Where is Prashanto? We are both from Calcutta. What will I tell his mother"? Any amount of cajoling won't help. So, we waited a bit and sure enough Prashanto appeared along with the last group, bringing smiles on the face of Aloke Majumdar.

While the rest of the group took the shorter route back to the Academy, Partho Sarathy Roy, IFS, found it difficult to carry his 90-kilo frame-up the gradient. Wangdi suffering from double-dosage, *Chhang* and whiskey, was finding it difficult to coordinate his movements. So, I and Bramha, who were the only non-drinkers in the group, had to stay back and help these two guys. Obviously, the shorter route was out of question. Hence, we moved along the longer route, the motorable track. At regular intervals, a furlong or two, the two would beg for a short break. I and Bramha had to virtually drag Wangdi and Roy along. During one such break, when they were squatting on a rock, Bramha spotted leeches peeping out of the holes on their trousers created by the nasty slip. Wangdi seemed to be oblivious of the fact perhaps due to lack of sensation. Bramha had to use burning cigarette butts to stamp out the leeches.

At last we reached Happy Valley, dog-tired and badly needed a cup of tea. We entered a restaurant at the entrance of the Academy. Three of us wanted tea, but Wangdi ordered a coke. When we were half way through our tea, Wangdi suddenly got up and rushed out but not quick enough to avoid any nuisance. When we came out Wangdi was gone. Next morning, when we met at the Academy, he innocently inquired, "Mukherjee, I am told someone committed nuisance at the restaurant"?

The rule of prohibition at Mt Abu couldn't dampen the spirits of the young police officers. Saturday nights were earmarked for 'Paploo' (cards) and cocktails. Gulab, a local brew made from rose petals, was a great hit. In addition, one or two probationers were despatched to Jaipur on holidays to bring crates of whiskey/beer/rum. The ex-army lot preferred rum. By this time, the novices had graduated and were careful enough to avoid embarrassing situations. Even then, there were stray incidents of people falling sick. In one of the rare incidents, a probationer, getting up in the middle of the night to answer calls of nature, mistook the wardrobe as the bathroom. Then there was Eric Ekka, Manipur, who strayed into a marriage reception at the *bazaar* after dinner and returned only next morning.

Chapter – 4

Snippets and Facets
'Rigorous Training'

The brief stay of about three weeks at Nagpur which covered short courses at the National Civil Defence College, Chief Inspectorate of Explosives and the National Fire Services College, was a welcome break after the hectic schedule at Mussorie. The routine left a lot of free time, the climate was very comfortable and there were plenty of cinema theaters at walking distance. The casualness of life here, however, left us unprepared/under-prepared for the change that awaited us at Mt Abu. Starting from the terrain, everything seemed different. The rugged and dusty landscape at Abu Road was in sharp contrast with the cool greenery of Mussorie.

At Dehradun, we had been received by a mild natured and smiling Gaekwad, incharge of physical education, and the journey to Mussorie covered in taxis in batches of three or four. The reception at Abu Road was rather lukewarm with a grim faced giant figure (6 ft 4 in) Assistant Sub Inspector Mishraji waiting to herd us into a police lorry. On a cold evening (3.12.71), we reached Rajputana House, our abode for the next one year. The privileged group of eight whom we used to refer to as Lords or Maharajas, found their accommodation in 'Jodhpur House' much cosier. The trans-shipment from Nagpur was in two batches. One batch had arrived at Mt Abu the previous day. They had lined up on the verandah for the regimental hair cut (also known as zero cut). People who sported fancy hairstyles looked rather morose. VK Mehta, very fond of his long hairs, was virtually in tears.

Next evening, we were asked to fall in at the Academy Square for initiation. After the usual sermons on discipline, hard work and good conduct, the batch was split up into five squads and made to march through the streets of Mt Abu up to the officer's mess. The regimentation had begun the first day itself. If I am not mistaken there were 65 of us, including two trainees from Bhutan, one from Sikkim, two Dy SPs from Manipur, two from Tripura and one from CBI. The IPS contingent included eight ex-army officers. The first day itself produced a casualty. The lone CBI officer, scared of the rigours lying ahead, packed up his baggage and said good-bye.

The physical component of the training proved rather taxing, especially in the first month. Knocking against the wooden horse during vaulting exercise and falls from the real horses were very common. A few suffered injuries during rock climbing as well. Balan Nair (who became DGP of UP) slipped down a cliff and badly bruised his palms. I had a crack in the right little finger from basketball and had to put on a plaster. During basketball again, Dhruv Mishra leapt for the ball and dug his nails in the forehead of Upendra Verma, missing the ball altogether.

There used to be a beeline to the dispensary, with people seeking parade exemption. This trick used to be very common with people, who got delayed for parade, generally due to oversleeping and hangovers. There were many cases of genuine nature also. Hardly, anyone escaped from blisters after the road walk and run and this was in spite of the precautions taken as per the advice of the drill instructors. Each one of us must have emptied half a pack of talcum powder into our socks for cushioning effect. Then there was the day we returned from long range firing with prominent abrasions on our shoulders. It became very difficult to do the push-ups.

The most exciting and interesting episodes were the ones scripted at the riding square. The common brickbats at every session, used to come from the instructors Hanuman Singh (later Janak Singh) and Gurcharan Singh, *"Saab, ghodi nahi samhalti hai, zila kaise samhaloge?* They used to narrate tales about the previous batches. One oft-repeated story was about a 1968 batch officer. When the instructor would give the command Mount! He would repeat the same to the syce—"Mount, Mount!" The syce would point out, *"Saab! Yeh command aapke liye hai"*. The probationer would mount reluctantly, but jump off and start trotting along with the horse the moment the 'Trot' command was given. The instructor would shout –*"Kya Saab, aap utar gaye"?* He could reply, *"Kya karoon? gira diya ghodi ne"*. Hanuman Singh would lament, *"Aise to aap riding kabhi nahi seekh payenge"*. The officer would promptly retort, *"Kya karoon? Jaan de doon kya"?*

No fingerprint is identical to another. The same applies to horses. They exhibited their own angularities. Some were insolent, some well-behaved, some lazy while others were hyperactive and difficult to control. There used to be a scramble among the probationers to grab the well-behaved ones. There was a horse called Raja, who used to trot diagonally. It was difficult to keep it in line with the other horses. Sundari was in the habit of lying down and rolling on her back, presumably due to an urge for itching. Janak Singh disclosed the reason only after I had a personal experience. For instructions, the riders will be asked to form a semi-circle with the horses in a standing position. During one such session, I suddenly found myself losing altitude and Janak Singh screaming, *"Ghodi giri, ghodi giri"*! (The horse is falling). Soon my boots hit the ground and I jumped out of the saddle. Sundari started rolling vigorously on her back. It stopped after a minute. Kanchan Singh, our drill instructor, commented from the sidelines, *"Yeh ghodi hai ya gadhi*"? (Is it a horse or a donkey). Janak Singh was not amused. He was more concerned about the safety of the saddle and kept on howling at me for the possible damage to it. However, he also gave a tip for future guidance–not to loosen the reins of the horse while in a stationary position.

Assistant Director KS Rathore hailed from a Princely State and was a reputed rider. He had avid interest in horses and in fact used to possess a personal stable housing some quality breeds. Govinder Singh, popularly known as Goofi, perhaps had some previous exposure to riding and used to appear confident unlike the majority of us, who were shaky in the beginning. So far so good. But Goofi won't stop with that. He would keep bragging about his equestrian ability and went to the extent of challenging KS Rathore. He readily accepted the challenge and organised a simple competition during one of our evening classes. While the rest were having lessons in 'Trot', the two challengers were engaged in an endurance test. They had to simply go on circling the ground in "Trot" mode, but without using stir-ups. The match went on for hardly two to three minutes. Suddenly, there was a thud and Goofi was on the ground. He put on a sheepish smile and joined the rest of us. Mr Rathore rode away silently.

A month before the final equestrian exam the batch was divided into two groups—the strong riders and the weak ones. There were extra classes for the second group. These classes were held in the polo ground in the evenings. There were about 20 of us. One evening, Gurcharan Singh was taking the class. Manoranjan Sinha was finding it difficult to restrict his horse—Chameli—to a standstill position when the briefing was going on. Gurcharan Singh yelled, "*Sinha Saheb, mai dikhata hoon ghodi kaise sambhali jatee hai.* Sinha Saab, dismount! Rajgopal Sahab, mount!" Perhaps Gurcharan Singh thought that Rajgopal was the strongest of the weaks. He felt flattered and mounted with a victorious smile. Neither the elation nor the smile was long-lived. In a flash of a second Chameli bolted with the helpless rider making feeble attempts to stop it. The horse and the rider disappeared from the polo ground and Gurcharan Singh had to gallop behind. Soon the horse cooled down and stood still.

Such incidents were not confined to weak riders alone. Dhruv Mishra happened to be grouped with the strong ones and moreover he considered himself to be a super one at that. During the course of our training, some new horses were purchased. These had to be acclimatised and were not available to the probationers. The instructors often used to talk about a mare Nargis that was rated as the best. Mishraji was keen to have a ride on that horse. Janak Singh tried to caution him repeatedly that he would not be able to control the horse. Mishraji was bent upon proving his prowess. Janak Singh reluctantly allowed him to use the horse for the jumping exercise. This event consisted of three consecutive jumps. The horse took off from the starting point in a flash. The first jump saw Mishraji losing his stirr-ups. After the second, he was seen lying on the horse back in a position parallel to the ground and by the end of the final jump his touch down was complete.

During one of the sessions, Bhullar sprained a knee as his riding boot slipped out of the stirr-up while mounting. He obtained six weeks parade exemption and was found sporting a kneecap. The walking appeared a bit laboured. Around that part of the year, Acharya Rajneesh used to have a camp at Mt Abu. Lot of curiosity was generated amongst the probationers about the activities in the camp. We were allowed to visit the camp one evening. The camp was situated on a site along the highway to Abu Road and at a distance of two to three kilometres from our mess. We walked the distance with Bhullar in the forefront. The visit was a rather disappointing one. All that we could see was a mass prayer session in which the guru was exhorting the devotees and the latter, including many foreign nationals, jumping up and down in a frenzy and chanting some unintelligible monosyllables. There were many spectators perched on the small rocks around. On looking around all the enthusiasm vanished in a flash. Mr Pratt, Asst Director (outdoor), giving a cold stare at Bhullar. One can easily guess the fate of the parade exemption.

Although the group returned disappointed but Majumdar didn't lose heart. He made friendship with a couple of volunteers and once was able to sneak into the bathing area with his camera on a Sunday morning. Subsequently, he made good use of the Academy studio and came out with stunning photographs for which there was great demand from the probationers as well as the officers attending the senior course. The driving classes were no less exciting. The long drives past Dilwara on the way to Achal Garh and Guru Shikhar and circling around Nakki Lake were really enjoyable. Rajendran was in the habit of looking at the knob while changing gears and in the process, would lose the bearing and the jeep would move towards the embankment. The instructor Jamedar (ASI) would grab the steering wheel and steady the vehicle in the nick of the moment.

A difficult exercise was to start the vehicle on an incline without sliding back. Two methods were taught–one was the half-clutch way and the other to use the hand brake. One day, after starting from the incline Sree Kumar was driving happily, gloating over his success. But to the horror of co-passengers the vehicle was moving only at 10 km per hour even on the plain road. People could feel the unusual heat generated by the wheels. The instructor had a quick survey and found out that the hand brake was on.

At the end of the training session, we had to appear for a test before the Sub-Divisional Magistrate of Mt Abu for obtaining the licence. The test comprised of a figure of eight, and stopping the vehicle on a slope after climbing it in reverse gear. In fact, the slope happened to be the entrance to the residential bungalow of the Deputy Director Administration. Dubey was perhaps in a tearing hurry to grab his licence and in the process, nearly missed the track. When he halted, the Magistrate observed smilingly, "The licence is being given to you for saving the lives of people and not otherwise". To another probationer, he commented that it is better he doesn't drive even after securing the licence. I suppose all of them turned out to be good drivers later.

Our mess at Rajputana House also witnessed some interesting episodes. The protocol and attendant code of conduct at dinner nights/mess nights appeared rather suffocating. The dining hall was a long rectangle. In the center of the hall there was a small projection at right angles, which could be called a subsidiary hall. This space could accommodate a table for 8 persons. The chief guest, members of the faculty by rotation, used to occupy the seat at the head of the table in the main hall. Consequently, those sitting in the subsidiary hall went out of the line of sight and enjoyed some freedom. At least violation of table manners will not be taken note of by the chief guest. Thus, there used to be great demand for a seat in the subsidiary hall, leading to a scramble. Only the early birds could make it. Maniram was a permanent member of this club of eight. However, on one of the occasions he was a bit late and lost his place. Reluctantly, he took a seat in the main hall. As usual the first item was soup with bread. Slices used to be kept piled up in centre plates and the diners had to transfer the required number to their individual side plates. Good manners warranted a limited intake, one or two slices only. Even before the chief guest had touched the slices Maniram had already grabbed a bunch of seven to eight slices and piled them in his plate. However, he could not straightaway make use of these since he had to wait for the butter tray. Suddenly, he realised that there was a murmur around and the gaze of all diners focused on his plate. He glanced at other plates and realised his indiscretion. Directing a frightful look towards the chief guest and constantly monitoring the latter's response (praying that his eyes escaped Maniram's movement) slowly started taking the slices one by one and putting them back quietly to the center plate. He was lucky enough to escape comments from the chief guest who happened to be the Deputy Director Administration. He only had handled our class on table manners and naturally was rather fastidious about them.

Mishraji was a body-builder and a voracious eater. He was very particular about a sumptuous breakfast. After marching back from the parade ground we used to walk straight to the mess in our parade dress. While others would cover the distance from the gate of Rajputana house to the mess leisurely, Mishraji would double up. We soon discovered the reason for his great hurry. The neighbouring plates would be empty with all the cornflakes transferred to Mishra's plate. Same would be the fate of the milk intended for both the neighbours. The heap of cornflakes in Mishra's plate would look like a mount, which would be difficult for a cat to jump over. The intake of bread and butter was commensurate with the quantity of milk and cornflakes. The magnitude of the consumption naturally had to reflect in the output and day after day CD Kainth, Mishra's roommate, would crib about the inadequacy of the number of thunder boxes since Mishra would use Kainth's box also.

The Academy square and the polo ground where parades were held had their own quota of anecdotes. People used to be pulled up as a matter of routine for turning up unshaved. Attempting to snatch some extra sleep they had to miss this imperative requirement before turning up for parade. SK Guha and PKB Chakravarty could never resist the temptation of munching a *paan* (betel leaf) on their way to the games period in the evening in spite of being hauled up everyday. One morning, Kamal Kumar turned up at the Academy square, a good ten minutes late. The parade had already started. Mr Pratt, Assistant Director (outdoor) growled, "Why are you late"? Kamal Kumar maintained his nerve and replied coolly, "I had been to the polo ground under the impression that the parade is being held there". Mr Pratt growled back, *"Dacoity Allahabad mein aur sahab chale Lucknow"*. (The dacoity took place in Allahabad and the officer proceeded to Lucknow).

No segment of Mt Abu chapter will be complete without Mishraji. We will always remember his way of commanding squad drill. We read about *rigor mortis* in forensic medicine.

There was no need for any practical demonstration at the mortuary. Mishra's countenance while hurling words of command was good enough to give us an idea as to what *rigor mortis* looks like.

Pradhan of Sikkim was another interesting personality. During a practice session at the short range he happened to be my adjoining shooter. While I was trying to concentrate on the target, suddenly the instructor (Mr Phansupkar) pounced on Pradhan to reset the nozzle of the revolver towards the target and yelled, "You nearly killed your fellow probationer". Nevertheless, Pradhan's callousness helped me in a great way during the firing with .22 rifles. My marks got boosted as he kept on firing merrily at my target.

Pradhan was fond of one of those pleasures of life. During our brief halt at Delhi on Bharat Darshan, he and VK Hansuka requested me to join them for lunch. We took a taxi from our place of stay in Kingsway Camp and proceeded to Connaught Place. The two were in desperate need for a prelunch session of beer. They picked up their stock at Connaught Place, but couldn't locate a suitable jaunt to relax and dispose of the same. They decided to go around the city to cover the session while on the move. Finally, we touched down at a *dhaba* near ISBT for lunch. There was a prolonged discussion over the menu and Pradhan came out with his serious suggestion. "Let us order two full chickens. Then we can have eight leg pieces". Initially, Hansuka nodded in agreement and kept on smiling silently. Suddenly, he realised the impossibility of the proposal and flared up, "You nut! You want to have eight legs from two chickens"? Pradhan climbed down his stand with amazing alacrity and settled down on the expeditious disposal of the leg pieces made available.

Cultural programmes also had their own share of amusement as well. BN Sashidhar was very particular about rendering a famous lullaby of KL Saigal on every occasion—"*So jaa, Rajkumari, so jaa*". So, the batch started calling him Rajkumari.

In one of the programmes Mishraji ventured to put up a one act play. He himself was the actor, director and playwright. It was a dialogue between Chanakya, the mentor of Chandra Gupta Maurya and Helen, Daughter of the Greek General Selukos, who married Chandra Gupta. Mishra donned the role of Chanakya. After lot of pleadings, Mrs Dutta wife of an officer attending the senior course, agreed to play the role of Helen. Mishraji had made meticulous preparations for the play. However, his make-up man was not careful enough. He did not bother to check up whether the wig was properly fixed on Mishraji's hair. With his deep involvement in the play Mishraji started overdoing the gestures while delivering his lines. The wig slowly started parting company with the natural hair on the frontal side. With every shake of the head the gap kept increasing. Gentle smiles started giving way to ripples of laughter. Fazed by the oddity of the situation Helen (Mrs Dutta) forgot her script and stood dumb for a couple of minutes. Shortly, thereafter she bolted from the stage, leaving Chanakya (Mishraji) alone with his wig dangling from the scalp. He withstood all the embarrassment, maintaining his composure throughout and then slowly walked off the stage. The audience kept rolling in their seats for long thereafter.

We had to get our winter dinner jackets (black and black) at Mussorie itself. At Mt Abu we were told that summer jackets (white and white) were required for attending mess nights and dinner nights. Options were given to stitch in terry cotton or plain cotton. In view of the limited use of the summer dinner jackets many probationers went for the cotton variety and Mishraji was one of them. Perhaps there were some defects in the stitching which did not escape the notice of the Deputy Director Administration. He made a harsh comment which upset Mishraji badly. Immediately, after dinner he walked down to the market to confront the tailor. Posing a menacing look he shouted, "Are you a tailor"? The non-plussed tailor could somehow manage to utter, "Yes". "Did you stitch this dinner jackets"? growled Mishra. Again the tailor meekly replied in the affirmative. Mishra promptly unbuttoned his coat and flung it at the tailor. With only trousers on, he was not sporting any vest and hands on his hips he kept on staring at the tailor to the amusement of a curious crowd that had collected impromptu. A fellow probationer who had accompanied Mishraji pacified him and brought him back to the mess after putting on the jacket.

The cadre allotment came as a mixed bag for the batch. Those who got their home states were happy, those who got accommodated in neighbouring states were not unhappy and those dispatched to far away states distinctly upset. Out of three officers allotted to Tamil Nadu one was an insider and the others from Delhi and Patna respectively. Both the outsiders had reasons to be upset. However, quickly they got over the situation and started concentrating on the language. After a couple of months they started muttering some common words and even simple sentences. Mr Padmanabhan of Kerala cadre attending the senior course was an effective teacher.

As the exams got completed and the preparations for the passing out parade began the probationers started discussing their prospects in the respective cadres. One evening after the second peg one of the allottees to a southern state started fantasising his reception in the state. He mumbled, "*State me jayegaa, CM se milegaa. Bolegaa–CM sir, vanakkam!* Bring me some whisky". The officer never told us his experience of the first meeting with the CM. I presumed it must have been a pleasant one as the latter found the officer suitable enough to head the force one day".

From Mt Abu to Vellore, Police Training College, the faculty-trainee relationship underwent a sea change. At Mt Abu the howling at the Parade Ground and the riding square notwithstanding there was no action on the part of the instructors that could hurt the sense of pride of a probationer. There was a constant feeding of the idea that each one of us was being groomed to be a leader. At Vellore, the entire approach was to puncture the ego instilled in the trainees at NPA. Right from the principal up to the instructor havildars none was an exception to this approach, barring a couple of law instructors. One of them was inspector V Manikkam, who used to be referred to as *Pacchai tannir* (plain water) Manikkam in view of his honesty.

To begin with, we were asked to join the parade squads of SI cadets. To boot, shoulder badges were not permitted. Fault finding was invariably accompanied by sarcastic comments from the principal, such as, "You can't even do a butt salute properly? Can't jump this wall? Even my daughter can do it". What was hurting was the fact that these comments used to be hurled in the presence of the SI cadets and instructors. Some of us had problem in crossing obstacles. They bore the brunt. Tensed up with fear of possible comments they used to take off in desperation. One used to invariably land in the water while attempting to jump across the water pit. Another had the problem of clearing the wooden horse. At Mt Abu, we were taught to vault over the horse by placing the hands on the horseback and swinging the body across through the arms. At Vellore, the exercise was a bit modified. We were required to jump over the horse and land up on a mattress after doing a front roll. Our fellow probationer Sahasranaman landed the rough way and broke his right hand. Of course, that earned him reprieve from the PT classes for the rest of our stay at PTC. All these incidents evoked only a derisive grin on the principal. The latter was a rank promotee and carried an understandable load of prejudice against directly recruited IPS officers. Hardly a day would pass without a glimpse of what he thought of IPS probationers. Occasionally, he would remind us that our careers were at his mercy. It was good fun listening to his megalomania. Most incomprehensible were his outbursts for imaginary breach of conduct rules. On a Sunday, the DIG in-charge of training stepped in our mess to join us for lunch. The principal thought that it was a crime for me to have been in mufti on the occasion. My understanding was that calling on in uniform was meant for official purposes. The howling by the old man after the departure of the DIG dispirited me so badly that I wanted to call it quits that day itself. However, my fellow probationers pacified me and made me change my decision.

On another occasion, we were wholly engaged in the mess on a Sunday, preparing for the departmental tests. That evening, there was a hockey match between the PTC team and a local outfit. There was no instruction that attendance at the match was mandatory. The defeat of our team enraged the principal and he singled out the three IPS probationers for giving vent to his anger the next day. We struggled hard to comprehend how our (only three of us) failure to turn up for cheering the team could be the sole cause of its defeat.

Cajoled by the instructors, who incidentally sailed in the same boat as us, we hung on and four months passed off pretty quickly. The old man tried to make amends by hosting a tea party on the eve of our departure for practical training, but perhaps it was too late to win our hearts.

Chapter – 5

Language Blues

Language Problems in my First Posting

My first posting was at Cheyyar, a quiet little sub-division in the erstwhile North Arcot district with Vellore as head quarters. There I had to suffer several tense moments while travelling in the office jeep, thanks to some incorrigible traits of the driver, Krishnamoorthy. Whenever he used to spot a woman on the road, he would keep looking at her and in the process lose his bearing. The vehicle would go off the track and the fellow will realise when the jeep is about to roll down the flanks and somehow would retrieve the situation in the last moment. I had to encounter such incidents day after day.

One of the days proved not to be so lucky. After attending Chief Minister's *bandobast* duty at Vellore I could return to Cheyyar at around 1 am. Madras was about 106 km from Cheyyar and due to time constraint I had to travel by the jeep as against the earlier plan of taking a bus. I had to reach Madras by 9 am to attend the Tamil Nadu Public Service Commission exam in Tamil. At the outskirts of Kanchipuram, the inevitable happened. While enjoying the sight of women, Krishnamoorthy lost control of the wheel and trampled upon some fowls. Raw in service, I got scared and asked him to drop me at the bus stand, report the incident to the police station and return to the headquarters.

Luckily, I could get a bus immediately and make it to the exam hall just in time. In spite of all the tension of the morning I was fortunate enough to clear the Tamil exam in the first attempt and in the process, bag three advance increments. Other North Indian officers were not so lucky and many had to wait for sometime for their senior scale. At the Public Service Commission I heard many interesting tales about the encounters these officers had in the interview board.

Most interesting of these encounters was narrated by a very senior officer, who, way back in the early sixties was posted as ADC to the Governor. Prior to this, he was posted as ASP in Tuticorin.

This officer used to make his narration absolutely captivating with dramatic gestures. He would go on—"Those days the Agriculture Secretary used to be the examiner for Tamil. One day, he happened to be summoned by the Governor. He came perspiring out of anxiety, trying to guess the subject matter. I made him comfortable and said -Don't worry, sir! Perhaps His Excellency needs some coconut saplings to be planted. After the meeting the Secretary came out relaxed and I thought this was my best opportunity. As he got into the car and closed the door I shoved my head in through the window and pleaded -Sir! I am again coming tomorrow! The Secretary queried, What for young man? I meekly submitted, For that half yearly trip I have been making to the Public Service Commission, sir"! Prompt came the reply -No, no, young man! I am not the examiner this time. I thought my last chance was gone and I would have to continue as the senior most ASP in South East Asia till eternity. The Secretary saw the despair in my eyes and said -Don't worry officer! I shall talk to my friend who is the examiner this time.

"With a faint ray of hope I reached the Public Service Commission next morning. The Chairman of the Board asked me to go through the contents of a letter and narrate the gist. I read it twice, thrice, scratched my head and started - Sir, this is a petition about a case of assault. Promptly, the Chairman stopped me - No, no, officer! This is a casual leave application. My heart nearly stopped –I had lost the last chance. But, you know? With all that I passed because I happened to be ADC to the Governor".

Another incident attributed to a non-Tamil officer messing up the language relates to a law and order situation in Madurai district. The SP left Madurai with his striking force on receipt of a message regarding a case of rioting. On the way, a village shandy was going on. On spotting the crowd from a distance, the SP asked the driver "*Enna ithe*"? (What is this), the driver replied "*Ayya, ithe santhai*". (Sir, this is a shandy). The SP mistook the word 'santhai' as 'sandai' (quarrel). He thought this was the place where rioting was going on and ordered the force to disperse the crowd.

Another interesting episode concerning a North Indian officer struggling to grapple with the language is about an IAS officer appearing before the Public Service Commission and saying "I don't know" to each and every question. In sheer exasperation, the examiner exclaimed, "Youngman, tell us one single word of Tamil you know". Prompt came the reply, "Sir, I know what banana is called in Tamil". The eyes of the examiner lit up and he encouraged the probationer –"Yes, yes. Please tell us". Without batting an eyelid the examinee proceeded, "It is *Villupuram*". Obviously, he meant *vaazhaipazham* (Banana). The examiner sank in his chair. This officer quickly managed a cadre change to avoid learning Tamil.

Another faux pas with the language was reported about an ASP. As soon as he entered the camp office, he asked the camp clerk to bring a fountain pen (pena in Tamil) for signing the charge report. Unwittingly, the following words came out, "*Penn kondu vaa*". (Which in Tamil means –'bring a girl'). Immediately, the camp clerk started circulating the words how immoral the new ASP was.

Talking about the language one recalls an incident of a different type. This was related to a correspondence between two Tamil speaking officers. One was the DIG in charge of Prohibition and the other a DySP, Prohibition in Tanjavur. The DIG had issued an order that all weekly reports be written in Tamil. This DySP had conducted a raid in a particular village and effected seizure of a substantial quantity of toddy. When the DIG saw the relevant entry in the weekly report, he remarked, "*Ivvazhavu kallu thideer enru engerenthu vanthathu*"? (Suddenly, where from this amount of toddy came)? The intention of the DIG was to check up why no toddy cases were detected from this area earlier. The spirit of the query eluded the comprehension of the DySP and he drafted a raw literary reply, "*Ayya! Ivvazhavu kallu panay marattilrendu vanthathu*". (Sir, this toddy came from the Palmyra tree). This prompted the DIG to observe further –"*Nallathu, inimel kallu koyya marattilrendu varavum*". Good, hereafter toddy will come from guava trees).

Chapter – 6

Police – Industry Interface

Trail of Encounters in Posting

Although I spent a year and half at my next sub-division, Neyveli, South Arcot, there was hardly any extraordinary event. But, life here started with an unpleasant experience in connection with a lock-out in Seshasayee Industries (insulators), Vadalur. Local Inspector, Ramachandran and Sub Inspector Venugopal disappeared when the employees, about 1000 in number marched to the company's guest house, leaving me and the Neyveli Town Sub Inspector Nagrajan with just a couple of sections of armed reserve to handle the situation. Luckily, nothing untoward happened and the employees left the guest house after much persuasion.

This experience of being ditched by the subordinates was in contrast to an incident that I had the opportunity to encounter in the first week of my posting at Cheyyar. Sometime in the second week of February, 1974 the then DIG Northern Range, Pon Paramaguru, had come to the district HQ Vellore. I was required to call on the DIG and left Cheyyar in the rickety old Bedford van. After crossing Arcot, I found the DySP Ranipet, P Pandian, with an Inspector, couple of SIs and a handful of local policemen standing on the main road opposite Melvisharam College. The field between the college and the village looked like a battlefield. I asked the driver to stop and inquired about the problem.

It seems the villagers got enraged due to some girls being teased by the students. Many of these students had rented out accommodation in the village. Their belongings were dumped on the road and set on fire. Villagers were armed with sticks and were hurling stones at the boys. The latter were also retaliating. I offered to help and suggested to the DySP that we should intervene. He was of the opinion that we should not enter the field without sufficient strength. He had given a message to the SP for sending armed reserve and the same was awaited from Vellore. I submitted that we should do something to prevent bloodshed and volunteered to enter the field. The Inspector, SIs and the handful of local policemen came along and the DySP also had to join. We stood like a buffer between the two warring groups, with missiles flying over us. We held on for about fifteen minutes, trying to persuade both groups to retreat. Soon, the SP and the Collector arrived with the striking force and we managed to make both the groups withdraw, thereby preventing a direct clash and resultant injuries.

The college was declared closed and the students escorted to safety through public transport. Though the incident at Vadalur showed the local officers in poor light it brought out the valliant in the Sub Inspector Nagarajan of the neighbouring police station, who stood beside me like a rock in the midst of the crisis.

The Vadalur incident reminds me of something of a lighter nature while I was at Neyveli. To promote healthy activities amongst the men I had put up a volleyball court in the sprawling campus of the town police station. Most of the evenings, I was able to snatch an hour's leisure and join the men at volleyball. The Inspector and the SI also used to join.

I had received an anonymous complaint that gambling was going on in a club in Mandarakuppam *bazaar* located on the Cuddalore-Vriddhachalam road. I wanted to take the organisers by surprise. Further, I doubted the bona fides of the local police. Hence, without giving any advance intimation, I huddled all the men along with the Inspector and SI into the van as soon as the game was over and directed the driver to proceed to Mandarakuppam. We reached the club within twenty minutes and stormed it. A local functionary of the ruling party was running the club. I spotted one of the inmates rushing out and running on the road. With all the muscles toned up after volleyball and sports shoes on, it was not difficult to launch a chase. With the entire crowd in the market watching, I felt like Milkha Singh and didn't realise that I had overtaken the person I was supposed to apprehend till I heard a commotion. Looking back I saw the man cornered by the Sub Inspector following behind. The raid was a grand success and the club had to close down following a rift between two factions of the ruling party. The police received copious encomiums.

Being an industrial township Neyveli offered problems of its own. Apart from labour agitations triggered off at the drop of a hat, accidents in the industrial area handed out experience of a different sort. Prevention of these mishaps called for a comprehensive policy on industrial safety and was the responsibility of the management. The problem that we faced was the common demand for dispensing with post-mortem examination. Every time we had to labour hard to convince the union leaders on the plus points in going for autopsy. Two common grounds on which I used to harp on were:

1. The dismembered body will be presented in an integral form after post-mortem, and
2. It would facilitate in processing insurance claims.

Two of the ghastly accidents are still vivid in my memory. One relates to an engineer being crushed under a crane, which capsized while being operated in the lignite mine. Here a different kind of problem cropped up with the Deputy Superintendent of Mines questioning the authority of the police in taking up investigation under Section 304 A of Indian Penal Code. According to him, the matter was covered under the Industries Act and the police had no jurisdiction. After prolonged deliberation, he gave in and allowed the investigation to be taken to its logical conclusion. One evening, I received a message that there was a blast in the fertilizer plant and two persons had died. On reaching the scene, I had the biggest shock of my life. There was a corpse on the floor with the upper half of the skull lying about 20 ft away and grey matter splattered on the floor. One of the hands was hanging on from a gas pipeline above. It was a very nauseating sight and took me quite sometime to gather my composure.

Our probe revealed that maintenance work was being taken up on the ammonia pipeline and some welding was required. It was taken for granted by the welder that the ammonia supply was cut off and there was no residual gas in the pipe. Unfortunately, this had not been cross-checked and the pipe exploded the moment the welding torch was lit up. It was a serious violation of safety guidelines and the management learned the hard way.

The NLC management was suffering huge losses due to pilferage of mines equipment, especially, conveyor belts and construction material, such as, cement and iron rods. Lot of hardware merchants in Mandarakuppam were thriving on this pilfered material. It was an organised business carried out in connivance with the watch and ward staff. I was very worked up about this trade flourishing right under the nose of the management and the police. Any action at the originating end would have been the domain of the management and any direct intervention by the police would have led to labour problems and friction with the management. So, I decided to strike at the destination and organised a raid on the receivers at Mandarakuppam. Cases were registered under Section 102 CrPC and substantial quantities of conveyor belts and cement recovered. Recovery from a notorious receiver worked up to Rs 1 lakh which was a considerable amount in 1974. The inputs given by us led the management to tighten the security apparatus. The menace was curbed to a great extent, thanks to excellent co-operation and initiative of the then security officer JB Joseph, who incidentally, will be remembered as an outstanding athlete who participated in the Asian Games at Tokyo.

Sub-divisional police officers were required to conduct raids to detect prohibition offences, gambling cases, violation of Immoral Traffic Act and offences covered by other special and local laws. Neyveli Township had two important clubs functioning under its auspices – The Town Club and the Park Club. The latter was usually visited by senior executives while middle level and junior officers thronged Town Club. Information was received that card games were played for stakes. The crowd was more on salary days, especially in the Town Club. I surprised the club one evening and found a good crowd of junior executives and ministerial staff. One of them happened to be a union leader. Anticipating pressures from various groups I asked for charge-sheet to be filed the same evening. The management had a draconian service rule, which provided cashiering of employees involved in police cases. Tremendous pressure was mounted on the management to take a lenient view, but nothing could be done as long as the case was pending. Through the local minister the union leader applied political pressure and the employees also had the support of the management. The double pressure worked and the collector ordered withdrawal of prosecution. However, I deemed it to be the real reward of our work, when about fifty women, family members of the delinquent employees, gathered at my camp office to thank the police profusely for the action taken against their husbands, who were squandering a good chunk of their wages in gambling, neglecting their families.

My next target was the Park Club. However, I thought of an alternative remedy as a first step. One Saturday evening, when the Club was in full attendance, I left on a stroll up to the Club which was just a five minutes' walk from my camp office. I left instructions with my camp office writer to give a call to the Club after ten minutes and inform that ASP was coming. I positioned myself on a roadside culvert opposite the main gate of the Club. The weekend celebrations were in full swing. Hardly, a couple of minutes would have passed, suddenly, the music stopped and the lights went off, presumably after the call from my camp office. Soon thereafter the members started trooping out, getting into their cars and speeding away. Quietly, I walked back home. There was no further need of a raid.

Motivated by my gesture of rewarding the constables, who brought in such information they pumped up their level of alertness and started detecting cases with added gusto. PC 538 Selvaraj and another PC (I don't remember the name) one evening were on cycle patrol in the township area. Around 8 pm, they came across a locked house with about twenty bicycles and mopeds parked in the campus. They got curious and leaving his companion to keep a watch, Selvaraj went to the nearest telephone booth and called up the Inspector. The latter turned up in no time with his posse of men and knocked at the door. It was an NLC quarter allotted to a junior engineer. A blue film was being shown with the help of an eight mm projector. Rs 20 per head had been collected from the viewers. The operator escaped after jumping through the window. A few of the spectators also managed to give a slip. However, about ten persons got into the net. The projector and the film were seized along with the collected amount. The Inspector narrated the details over the telephone. I gave instructions for prompt chargesheeting of the case and depositing the case property in the court. Later I came to know that the court had returned the film and the projector to the police for safe custody. I learnt from the Inspector that following circulation of the news relating to the seizure there was great demand from the VIPs including the Magistrate, the Superintendent of Police, other police officers, and the Assistant Public Prosecutor to watch the film. Since the operator had been absconding the Inspector had to get the writer Head Constable

Muthukrishnan self-trained, through trial and error method. One of the VIP rooms in the Circuit House was used as a theatre.

This raid had the same nuances as the gambling case visa-a-vis, the NLC employees who ran the show and formed part of the crowd. Ultimately, all of them got away. However, the cases definitely had deterrence value and the sensation remained in the minds of the people for days to come.

Chapter – 7

Grounding as an Administrator

After a stint of around one and a half years at Neyveli, I got promoted as Superintendent of Police and posted to Dharmapuri. The order was received on the 21st of March, 1976. This was preceded by a short period of uncertainty. On the 30th of January, SP Cuddalore had informed me that my name had been proposed for the Nilgiris and orders were expected within a day or two. As luck would have it, President's Rule was promulgated the next day and more important matters were taken up by the new administration in preference to routine matters like the promotion of a Joint Superintendent of Police. There was consequent delay which in turn resulted in change of place of posting originally proposed. Instead of Ooty, I was to go to Dharmapuri. My wife was rather upset at the change, but I could manage to convince her that the place did not matter.

I handed over charge at Neyveli on the 22nd of March and left for Madurai with the idea of undertaking a pilgrimage to the temple city of Madurai, Rameshwaram and Kanyakumari during the joining time. I was to halt at Madurai and scheduled to have dinner with Ravi Armugham, Assistant Superintendent of Police, Tallakulam. At his house, I received a call from Hariharane, SSB II advising me to join immediately as there was a likelihood of the promotion being cancelled following two officers, who had been compulsorily retired during the emergency, returning on the strength of High Court orders. I cut short my tour and returned to Neyveli the next day only to pack up and leave for Dharmapuri early morning on the 25th of March.

Before receiving fresh orders for Madurai North as against Salem proposed earlier, my batchmate KP Jain, who was also to be promoted in the same order, had to wait for another three weeks on account of the rehabilitation of the two officers sent home earlier. One of them gave vent to his bitterness while closing his weekly report. He wrote, "After 26 years of meritorious service I am being sent out unceremoniously. This is sheer malice, but God is great."This was commented upon by the then police chief in the following words: "True! But some Gods are greater". The punished officer proved that he was right by winning the case in the High Court. It is said that the officer on return to duty got posted as commandant in one of the battalions. He ordered a ceremonial parade to mark his return. In the process of unfathomable fun and frolic he slept off. The parade which had fallen in at 0545 hours kept waiting till noon by which time the parade commander had to take a decision to march off the contingent. Imagine the contempt for the officer that would have cropped up amongst the rank and file.

This was a slightly embarrassing situation since Jain had to work with me till receipt of fresh orders. Anyway, being close friends and batchmates we knew how to tackle the situation. So, instead of he (Joint SP, Krishnagiri) coming to call on me, I reversed the drill and visited him at Krishnagiri the next day, when I went to call on the DIG Palanivelu. Those days, the Range Headquarters was at Krishnagiri. Within a few days the same was shifted to Vellore.

Jain and I have been the best of friends since our Mussorie days and the bonhomie continues till today. However, even now he nurtures a grievance, aired in a lighter vein before other batchmates, that I made him accompany me for a prohibition raid.

The tenure at Dharmapuri was mostly peaceful except two incidents which caused some anguish and anxiety. One was a ghastly accident at Kadathur on Good Friday when a customer picked up a quarrel with a retailer selling gelatin sticks and detonators. The clientele usually comprised of agriculturists, who had to use the explosives for deepening the wells. In the instant case, the customer was haggling with the shopkeeper over the price of gelatin sticks. Enraged over the latter's reluctance to reduce the price, the customer threw the stick on the floor. Accidentally, the stick hit the heap of the explosives. In the resultant blast, sixteen people lost their lives and many were injured. The impact was more as the shop was located in a congested area. The police station was located very near the scene of occurrence and allowed the trade without taking cognizance of the lack of safety parameters to be observed by the trader. The Sub Inspector was placed under suspension and a district wide operation launched to check the premises of all shops dealing with explosives.

The second incident was one, which marked the resurgence of left wing extremism in the district. A landlord by the name of Appasamy Chettiar was brutally attacked in Mathur police station limits and hacked to death by a group of Naxalites, led by Sivalingam and Seeralan. I took up the case as a challenge and personally supervised several combing operations. However, in view of the nature of the case, it had to be handled by a specialised agency located in the Special Branch, now known as Q Branch and the Inspector General EL Stracey advised me that I could continue my association with the case by providing logistic support. The case was detected by the Special Wing and the key accused Seeralan was arrested from a neighbouring village in Natrampalli police station in North Arcot district. Unfortunately, while being escorted to the police van there was a scuffle and the accused died. This gave an unpleasant twist to the case. There was a customary inquiry under PSO 145 (Police Standing Orders) followed by an inquiry by a member board of revenue. This led to the prosecution of the investigating officer and his team and departmental action against supervisory officers including two Superintendents of Police. Interestingly, one of them had nothing to do with the main incident as he was posted as SP North Arcot long after the encounter. His mistake was to have sent a report against the RDO for trying to influence the witnesses at the time of the second inquiry. Understandably, his report was found to be not true and he was served a charge memo. It is atrocious that this officer had to suffer for more than fifteen years on this count. In extreme anguish, he remarked one day that he would have completed the punishment even for murder earlier to the disposal of the charge memo. The pending disciplinary proceedings stood in the way of his career development for years.

While handling the case, I went through tremendous tension in the first few days. Mr Mohandoss, DIG, CID would call at least twice a day and find fault with our investigation. He would not give any specific input, but simply express his anguish over the delay in detection of the case.

I felt much relieved when the investigation of the case got transferred, but the ominous signal about the resurgence of Naxalite activity robbed my sleep in the days to come. The writing on the wall was clear and we had to pull-up our socks. Hence, massive combing operations were launched in the hills and jungles and the intelligence machinery geared up.

There was an interesting episode linked with the case. One afternoon, when I was attending to *tappals* (mail) in the camp office, I heard a transmission over the VHF, 'Mike 10' calling Mathur. As 'Mike 10' was the call sign of the SP, it was obvious that someone was trying to impersonate. I intervened immediately and asked Mathur police station not to respond. The ghost-caller again came on the line, "Mr Mukherjee! Be careful. Save your life". Wondering whether the extremists would have infiltrated the VHF network, I promptly initiated a report to the IGP. An investigation was ordered and soon radio technicians swooped on Dharmapuri. They tried to track the ghost station, but in vain. Under instructions from the Special Branch CID, security at my residence and District Police Office was tightened and I started carrying a 9 mm pistol. I knew that all this was unnecessary, as there could be a second possibility – someone playing a prank. As expected, I received source information that the caller was the wayward son of a DySP whose activities were under the scanner. Of course with the limited wherewithal those days the staff of the police radio branch was not in a position to confirm or deny this. However, my belief in this theory took the load off my mind and I resumed a normal life style, jettisoning all the extra security and the long list of dos and dont's prescribed by SB CID.

The rest of the tenure went off as smoothly as possible. In the meantime, we had undertaken to stamp out ganja cultivation in Chitteri hills and the hilly tracks of Denkanikotta. During these raids, we tumbled upon several illicit fire-arms, mostly single barrel breech or muzzle loaders. The ganja cultivators used to keep them to hunt or chase away wild animals. A district-wise campaign was launched and about 1360 such weapons were seized. Many of them bore metallic discs nailed on the butt in memory of the kills achieved.

These weapons were brought to the Reserve Stores in Dharmapuri DPO. Some people from Pudukottai museum came to inspect these weapons. A few of them were identified to be of Mysore war vintage and taken to the museum for display. The credit for organising this drive is largely attributed to the then DySP Dharmapuri, V Jeganathan.

The Parliamentary polls held in March, 1977 saw a change of guard at New Delhi. The election passed off peacefully including the pre and post election period. The Assembly elections were due in June. A general shuffle was expected before that. Sometime in April there was a short course to be attended by a select group of SPs at Police Training College, Madras. After the class, the group got divided into sub-groups for calling on the police chief. Our sub-group comprising C Dorairaj (1962 batch), SP Ramnad West, KP Jain (1971), SP Madurai North, D Mukherjee (the author) and Deepak Samal (1972) ASP, Hosur. Led by Dorairaj, we marched into the chamber of EL Stracey, IP.

The IGP referred to the general shuffle in the offing and was magnanimous enough to hear us on the subject. "Gentlemen, the die is being cast, any preferences"? He first looked at the senior most (Dorairaj). The latter submitted, "Sir, I am constructing a house in Madras and would like to be here". After ascertaining the stage of construction came a terse observation, "Well, I do not promise, but shall certainly consider". Next was Jain's turn. He was ready, "Sir, today only I completed one year in Madurai". The reply was not positive, "Well, I hardly completed one year at any place. What about you Muk?" I had picked up enough hint from the first two interactions and meekly submitted, "Sir, I will go to any place you send me". He smiled— "What about Madurai City"? "It is a nice place with some rural jurisdiction also". I simply nodded. The Chief hinted that we should leave—"Fine, gentlemen! See you then". The calling on was over in five minutes. Normally, this incident would not merit any special mention as it relates to a mundane administrative episode, but comparing the state of affairs prevalent today the interaction of the Chief with some SPs quoted here does appear extraordinary. One is amazed at the authority the Chief enjoyed those days. A young SP manning a district had come to adverse notice and the Chief suggested his shift to a battalion. The SP attempted to stall his transfer through political pressure. It is learnt that the Chief resisted even the CM's wishes and the latter relented. The young man was marched in orderly room and given a dressing down.

Most of the proposals of the IGP came through with a slight change in my case. After discussion with the IGP, the Government changed my posting to Tirunelveli. It was nice of the IGP to have called me up and informed about the change. His words sounded extremely pleasant when he said that Tirunelveli was the stepping stone for all officers dreaming to head the Tamil Nadu Police one day. It was also an act of kindness on his part to ascertain my convenience for joining at Tirunelveli. As agreed, I had to join on 07.05.77 and got relieved on 03.05.77.

Chapter – 8

Alerts Belied

Before proceeding to Tirunelveli I had to face a volley of advices and words of caution from colleagues, senior officers and people supposed to be my well-wishers. The common threat was the problematic nature of the district and how difficult was it to handle. Of course, we were already aware of the caste problems and their intensity and also a constabulary that had a reputation of being highly polarised on caste lines. Each advisor would narrate the aggressive protest by the armed reserve men belonging to a particular caste with angry outburst against the then district police administration. On 21.11.72 students of St John's, St Xavier's and MDT Hindu College took out a procession protesting against the policies of the state government. As the processionists turned violent, police resorted to a lathi-charge to control the situation. In the process, one Lourdhu Nathan, a student of St Xavier's College, jumped into Tampraparani River and got drowned.

The next day, the students and the agitating public attempted to carry the dead body through the important roads of the town. When the mob was nearing Palayamkottai market they could not proceed further as a police van had broken down. The Armed Reserve personnel got down from the van. At that time, the rifle of head constable Shankara Pandian went off accidentally. He sustained injury and died later.

The policemen thought that the shot came from the side of the mob. Sequel to this, there was some unrest among the policemen and they refused to attend duty. As the situation worsened, Senior Officers tried to intervene. Omission on the part of Senior Officers to visit the head constable in the hospital aggravated the situation and it required a visit by the IGP FV Arul to diffuse the crisis.

Still fresh in mind was the ghastly incident at Mathalapuram near Vilathikulam in which 18 Thevars were burnt alive to avenge the murder of Guruswamy Naickar, the panchayat president. During 1973, Duraisingam and others murdered one Vivek Naicker of Mathalapuram due to enmity and rivalry over panchayat elections. This case ended in acquittal although Guruswamy Naicker showed keen interest and assisted the prosecution.

The enmity perpetuated further and a complaint was lodged on 21.10.73 that two Thevars were chased by Guruswamy Naicker and party when the two were cutting trees. Since then they were found missing. The case was referred as undetected. Subsequently, it was reopened in 1976 at the instance of the Thevars. Hence, the rivalry between the two communities flared up and security proceedings were drawn against them. In 1974 also a Naicker was killed by three Thevars at Mathalapuram and the same was acquitted in spite of interest shown by Guruswamy Naicker.

The Thevars gave vent to their pent up feelings on the 4th of August 1976 by murdering Guruswamy Naicker right in the middle of Vilathikulam bazzar. The assassins Duraisingam and Sundaikai took the severed head and abandoned it in a field.

The Naickers of Mathalapuram retaliated, by burning 18 Thevars alive including women and children.

In view of this turbulent history of the district, I took charge with a sense of anxiety. The sheer workload was appalling. It was perhaps the largest district considering the expanse of the police establishment, with 79 police stations and 23 out-posts. During the crime meeting I found some inspectors standing in the corridor since there was not enough space inside my chamber. *Tappal* used to come in a jeep as compared to a motorcycle in most of the other districts. In case due to some law and order problem I could not attend to *tappal* on a day or two, they would pile up to such heights that the people could not see the SP working behind the heap of files. To dispose of the backlog I used to drive into the reserve forest guest house in Munnanthurai where there was no telephone to disturb me. Reaching the camp in the evening, I used to sit on the verandah and finish off the files by midnight. The ambience facilitated complete concentration. I would then go on a safari in a jeep to see wild life, which was in plenty those days. Returning to the guest house around 2 am I would hit the bed, get up in the morning and proceed to headquarters as fresh as morning dew. After my relief from the district a year later on deputation to CBI, I had to take a day off at Chennai, convert the retiring room at Egmore as my camp office only to complete the ACRs (Annual Confidential Reports of SIs and above). There were days when concentrating on the files in my camp office I would have lost track of time till the sound of the reville indicated that the parade was falling in.

Although the so-called well-wishers had succeeded in painting a grim picture of the district, I found the going fairly smooth with no instance of caste/communal murder, death in custody or police firing. The district force was professionally competent and rose up to each occasion, whether to maintain law and order or handle crime. All they required was a neutral administration.

The Assembly elections passed off without any serious incident. The IGP had forewarned me about possible violence and adoption of unfair methods in Sathankulam constituency and desired very firm steps to be taken on our part. On the prepoll day, the Collector and I were camping at Armuganeri. In the evening, we decided to take a round of the constituency. At the entrance to Nazareth town we spotted an ambassador car on the tank bund in a badly smashed up condition. The road was littered with broken glass pieces. Obviously, it was an act of hooliganism prompted by election rivalry. Immediately, we rushed to the police station and found the DMK candidate Nellai Nedumaran lodging a complaint relating to the attack. The Inspector Mr Vedakkan was present in the station. He enjoyed the reputation of being a tough cop and needed no motivation. I simply gave him a time frame - "I shall come back after a couple of hours. I want to see the culprits in custody by that time".

We went back to Armuganeri for dinner and when we returned, the Inspector surely had complied with the instructions. We patted him profusely. Next morning when we came to check up the progress of polling, a crowd of voters assembled at the panchayat office to thank the SP and the Collector for the tough action against the rowdies. Some of them even prostrated. I recalled the conversation with the IGP Mr Stracey a couple of days earlier to the polls. "There is a candidate in Sathankulam, who is likely to deploy musclemen with *aruvals* and *koduvals* to win the election anyway. I want you to be very firm in putting down this rowdyism. You should camp in the area, visit every village of the constituency and assure voters of adequate protection. As far as this election is concerned you are directly responsible to the IGP. You will not take instructions from anybody else. "The day after the polls when I called up the IGP to report compliance of his instructions he was indeed very happy".

The Collector V Sundaram took keen interest in police operations and used to volunteer to come along with me in most of the law and order situations. Following the demand for allowing formation of students unions in all colleges, an agitation started by late July. It commenced with Sadakaptullah College followed by MDT Hindu College and later spread to other parts of the state. There was violence in Sadakaptullah College on 2.8.77. I was camping along with the Collector at Kutrallam for Saral Vizha festival. When I reached the college the students were pelting stones and breaking the glass panes. The principal went into a huddle in his chamber and missiles were hurled targeting his room also. The local DySP with paltry strength was unable to control the mob. I immediately requisitioned sufficient AR strength. In the meantime, the Collector joined me and we went upto the terrace from where the Collector tried to pacify the students using a police megaphone. There was no respite and the violence continued unabated. In the meantime, the additional force had arrived and we could see them lined up behind the mob. I suggested to the Collector that we should use force. He readily agreed and I signalled to the column to advance and chase them off. The over-enthusiastic Collector started screaming in frenzy, "Chase them! Fire! Fire"! Luckily the force did only what was required. Most of the students bolted from the scene, leaving the ground littered with cycles, notebooks and chappals. These helped the police later in tracing the absconders. The action had a salutary effect and contained the problem in our district although it spread to other parts of the state. At MDT Hindu College we simply stood at the gate and after an hour or so the agitators dispersed on their own.

The only other incident of somewhat serious dimension relates to a rift between two groups of Muslims (Mangalasundari group and Pettai group) at Kadayanallur. A child had died in a family belonging to the Mangalasundari group and the Pettai group who were in control of the mosque, was refusing to permit burial in the ground belonging to the mosque. All negotiations coordinated by the Tahsildar and the Revenue Divisional Officer failed. The body was decomposing since thirty hours had passed and there was a crisis. Large number of people from Pettai group had congregated in the mosque to prevent entry by the other group. In consultation with the Revenue Divisional Officer, it was decided to use force to clear the crowd and arrange a quick burial under police protection. Use of force in a place of worship could have had serious repercussions, but to our good luck the Government of the day endorsed the police action in which a lathi-charge was given and several agitators were arrested. (about sixty-four of them). In fact, the radio message sent by the Collector formed the basis of the reply given in the Assembly which was in session at that time. The only intervention came in the form of a request for releasing the accused on bail as conveyed by the DIG Tirunelveli. Obviously, he must have received instructions from the CM's office.

Even in the midst of serious business, there was no dearth of comic relief in this otherwise hyperactive district. The first visit to the district by Dr MG Ramachandran after taking over as Chief Minister was sometime in early November 1977. The visit had to cover a marriage function, a party meeting arranged in a cinema hall and a public meeting in the evening after which he was to drive down to Kanyakumari district.

I left the marriage function to check up the security arrangements for the party meeting. The Collector followed suit. He was travelling in an open jeep. The moment the jeep screeched to a halt at the portico of the hall he jumped out in a show of agility. He was dressed up in an immaculate white ceremonial suit (Buttoned-up coat). Soon after jumping out his countenance changed and I could guess his discomfort. He whispered to me that his trouser had snapped at a vital point and it was not possible for him to continue with the programme. I decided to summon his car, and advised him to walk backwards to get into the car, go home, change over and come straight to the circuit house to meet the CM. I asked him not to bother about the party meeting. An embarrassing situation was overcome silently.

March 1977 saw a change of guard at New Delhi which had its own ripples reaching the states. Prabhudas Patwari replaced Mohanlal Sukhadia as the Governor of Tamil Nadu. During his first visit to Tirunelveli a function was organised to lay the foundation stone of a residential colony for retired defence personnel. The venue was Krishnapuram near Tirunelveli on the Tiruchendur road. At the entrance to the function place a group of twenty villagers was lined up with mud pots (used for distilling arrack) placed before them. While welcoming His Excellency they were scheduled to break the pots with the clubs provided and take a vow not to produce or drink alcohol again. However, there was a small slip on the part of the Revenue Officials. They had forgotten to brief the villagers on the slogans to be raised while breaking the pots. The show was organised to impress the VIP, who was a Gandhian and a strong advocate of prohibition.

The moment His Excellency alighted from the car; the group launched their operation in full gusto, shouting slogans they were familiar with, completely ignorant of the radical change in the political leadership with no clue about the political allegiance of the VIP being welcomed. They were screaming –"Indira Gandhi Vazhgal! Indira Gandhi Vazhgal". (Long live Indira Gandhi). The Governor appeared absolutely puzzled and simply looked at the Collector who in turn, found it convenient to scan the horizon for possible clouds which were nowhere in sight. As the Governor climbed up the dais the momentary embarrassment was forgotten much to the relief of the Collector.

On the 4th of October, 1977 Indira Gandhi was arrested by the CBI in New Delhi. This led to angry protests by Congress party workers all over the country. Tamil Nadu also witnessed sporadic incidents. As far as Tirunelveli was concerned, it was reported that a crowd had gathered on the main road at Kovilpatti and was compelling the shopkeepers to down their shutters. The police had to use mild force to disperse the unlawful assembly.

I rushed to Kovilpatti with the striking force and took stock of the situation. The tension had died down and things were under control. Leaving instructions for strengthening pickets and intensifying patrols I rushed back to the headquarters for monitoring the situation throughout the district. No untoward incident took place, but an alert message from the Collector camping at Madras provided the anti-climax. The message read –"Maintain law and order with fear or favour". Obviously, the word 'OUT' was left out inadvertently during transmission. Fortunately, all the Sub-Divisional Police officers had enough grey matter to identify the mistake and not get carried away by the letters of the message.

A narration of the Tirunelveli saga would be incomplete without mentioning one Krishna Menon; rank promoted DySP, who got posted to Tirunelveli Sub-Division soon after I joined. He was a very hard working and knowledgeable officer. One would like to remember him for his mannerisms as well. He was in the habit of repeating his utterances expecting the listener to complete the remaining portion. For example, while talking about an Assistant Sub Inspector in the Taluk police station he would assert, "Sir that ASI is a blaggard"! The next moment he would put the sentence in a question form, "That ASI is a"? I had to complete the sentence "Blaggard"! He would go on –"He is running a parallel police station. He is running a"? I had to repeat like a parrot- "Parallel police station".

The said Krishna Menon happened to be a member of the Constable Recruitment Committee of which I was the Chairman and the DySP Armed Reserve, Mr Krishnan being the other member. This was a marathon exercise and starting from six o'clock in the morning we finished the physical and written test by the end of the day. The *viva voce* was slated for the next day. However, the candidates pleaded that they would prefer to finish the interview in the night itself, as it will be difficult for them to go back to the village and come again immediately. The committee agreed to the proposal and the entire exercise was completed by day-break, selecting 250 candidates.

During the *viva voce*, I was putting questions pertaining to current affairs. Since Karnataka was in news at that time, I was asking the candidates as to who was the Chief Minister of Karnataka. After four or five candidates correctly mentioned the name of Devraj Urs, I felt that other candidates would have come to know by this time that this was a possible question. Accordingly, I decided to reframe the question and asked the next candidate - "Devraj Urs Yaar"? (Who is Devraj Urs?). The candidate had a good look sizing up all the three of us and coolly pointed his finger at Krishna Menon- "*Eevar thaan, sir*". (He only sir). Obviously, he must have been impressed by the appearance and energy level of Krishna Menon.

Krishna Menon was replaced by a young Assistant Superintendent of Police, R Natarajan (later changed his name to Nataraj), who got Tirunelveli as his first sub-division. His batchmate K Vijay Kumar got trained by me and went away to Nagerkoil. Throughout my tenure at Tirunelveli P Rajendran, destined to succeed me as the Chief, 30 years later, remained at Tuticorin. Another youngster K Bhaskar, DySP underwent training at Tirunelveli. Nataraj, Bhaskar and Sameer Vyas, Assistant Collector under-training were bachelors and staying together. All these three were very dear to me and received brotherly treatment. Same was my relationship with Vijay Kumar. Without detriment to any official work we used to group together over dinner and sometimes watch movies in theaters.

A set of cane chairs worth Rs 150 purchased from a cooperative society at Shencottah was my first acquisition. The consignment arrived around 11:30 pm. My wife and I agreed that there should be an inauguration. So, I called up the three musketeers Natraj, Sameer and Bhaskar and my wife quickly prepared tea and brought some ground nuts. At the stroke of midnight, the five of us sat on the lawn and gossiped till late night.

It was rather sad that Bhaskar passed away prematurely about twenty years later. He was an outstanding basketball player. Another officer of my Tirunelveli days, who had a premature death, was Shanmughanathan DySP Srivaikuntam. With his giant frame, he was known for adopting crude methods of policing which was in sharp contrast to his flair for extra-curricular activities such as music and magic shows. Once there was a group clash in Eral police station limits. After the requisite police action, a peace committee was formed and Shanmughanathan was to attend the same. Peace committees are set up to ease the tempers and find amicable solutions. Of course, during the course of free and frank discussions there might be exchanges. These are to be ignored and the rival groups made to agree to peaceful co-existence. In this case, Shanmughanathan added fuel to fire by trying to suppress the recalcitrant voices with the help of the stick. The very purpose of the peace committee was defeated and peace became a casualty. Telegrams were sent by the agitating villagers and the Additional SP had to be rushed to sort out the matter.

One evening Rajendran dropped in at my camp office for some consultations. I had asked Nataraj to come with me for the Kumbhabhisekham at Sankarankoil. The function was fixed at 5 o'clock in the morning and we had planned to halt there the previous night. I requested Rajendran to join us, but he pleaded that he had not brought any change for night stay as he was scheduled to go back to Tuticorin. I asked him to send a message to Tuticorin so that his clothes could be brought straight to Sankarankoil.

We reached the guest house at Sankarankoil around 2 am. Rajendran's box had still not reached. We badly needed to snatch some sleep. Rajendran could no longer wait for his mufti. He looked here and there and finally when his eyes fell on the bedspread he nearly screamed "Eureka". He quietly picked up the bed sheet, converted it into a lungi, hit the bed and started snoring. Recharged with that short rest we were ready in our khaki by 5 o'clock in the morning.

Chapter – 9

Entry in the Premier Investigating Agency

Hoping for a placement in my home town (Patna) I had expressed my willingness for a central deputation. The first response from the Ministry of Home Affairs was a slot as Commandant, Central Industrial Security Force, Durgapur in West Bengal. Mr Stracey was once again kind enough to check up my reaction. I pleaded with him that I would love to go to CBI. The gracious Chief bailed me out and I hung on at Tirunelveli till a pleasant surprise visited me in April 1978 with a message from the MHA requiring the Tamil Nadu Government to indicate my availability for CBI. After attending a very useful Management Development Programme at the National Academy of Administration, Mussorie I returned to Tirunelveli only for a few weeks, before being relieved on the 14th of June on deputation. I finally left Tirunelveli on the 25th of June and was scheduled to arrive at New Delhi by GT Express on the 29th June. As I was a stranger I required some assistance at Delhi and took the liberty of sending a mail to one of my senior officers who was already on deputation to CBI from Tamil Nadu, to help me in the trans-shipment from the station to my temporary abode in Delhi—Tamil Nadu House.

To my bad luck, the officer was on long leave and my request for help went unattended. With five huge boxes and two kids, four and two years respectively, I felt completely at sea. Leaving my wife to guard the children and the luggage, I had to stand in the queue for a taxi. Ultimately, we reached Tamil Nadu House and cramped ourselves in room number 212 where we felt very comfortable. However, we had to leave the accommodation after two months which was the maximum duration of stay permitted at a stretch.

With creature comforts at virtually zero level, life at Delhi proved to be a great leveller. There was no transport provided by the department for going to office and back. Lack of familiarity with the public transport system forced one to use three wheelers. A meagre Rs 3500 saved on the sale of my car before coming to Delhi got consumed in no time even though one could save money on the return journey by walking the distance from North Block to Tamil Nadu House.

The first day in CBI was the only exception as VR Laxminarayanan, TN Cadre, a senior Joint Director was kind enough to send his car to drop me at CBI head office. It was a badly needed help since I was dressed up in tunic (ceremonial dress). Those days that was the dress order in Tamil Nadu for calling on and raw from the district, I didn't bother to find out what was the dress order in CBI. Later, I learnt that it was lounge suit or buttoned-up coat. Although some senior officers passed snide remarks, as uniform was anathema to CBI, VR Laxminarayanan came to my rescue, mentioning the practice in Tamil Nadu. To my great surprise, John Lobo, Director had no comments on my dress. In fact, later I came to know through my DIG that he appreciated my calling on in ceremonial dress. More surprise awaited me as I got posted as his staff officer straightaway although the tradition in CBI was that a newcomer always got posted to a branch. The senior staff officer, AR Sridharan (Karnataka Cadre) who was my DIG, explained that my posting as AIG was in view of the impending CBI conference.

Even Joint Directors had to commute in their personal vehicles or use the public transport for coming to office. One of them G Ramachandran, later became DGP Gujarat, was pedalling his way to Patel Bhavan, CBI Head Office, from RK Puram. Personal use of official vehicles except on payment, used to be frowned upon. When I was posted in a Central Investigating Unit located in Loknayak Bhavan, Khan Market, the branch car used to be parked in the garage allotted in the earlier premises at East Block, RK Puram. At the end of the day, when the vehicle used to return to the garage, about four to five investigating officers working in Loknayak Bhavan used to get a ride up to the garage from where they used to walk down to their quarters nearby. Even this trivial matter became a subject matter of a probe which culminated in orders being passed to park the vehicle in Kota House (where the Admin Division was located) nearby, although there was no garage facility. The whole thing emanated from surveillance mounted on a particular investigating officer who was trying to form a union.

There were several dampeners on the personal front and some of them need to be narrated to highlight the tough life a junior officer had to lead at Delhi those days. From the sprawling bungalow of SP Tirunelveli with a six acres campus to a 12 by 10 feet room in TN House was indeed a big change. Immediately after joining, I had applied for an eligible accommodation. In spite of several visits to the Directorate of Estates at Nirman Bhavan, I could not evoke any favourable response from the Deputy Director concerned. In the meantime, the maximum period of two months permitted at Tamil Nadu House came to an end. I had started scouting for rented accommodation. One of the LDCs in the office offered his LIG flat at Rajouri Garden on rent, but my superior officer advised me to refrain from the transaction on grounds of propriety.

At last a contact from my hometown came to my rescue. He was working in the Ministry of External Affairs and staying at Niti Bagh with his uncle, who was a Supreme Court Advocate. A friend of theirs, who happened to be a counsel for the Government of Karnataka, had constructed a house in the neighbourhood. On top of the garage there was a servant quarter with a bed room, bath and kitchen attached. The staircase landed straight into the bedroom. There were no windows; these were substituted by a ventilator through which my wife and children used to look at the aircrafts approaching Palam, which was the only relaxation they had in that one month of quarantine. We had to sleep on the floor. Yet none complained.

In the next month, there was a conference during which I met Shantanu Sen, SP CBI Calcutta. He was surprised that I did not even have a transit accommodation allotted by the Estates although more than two months had passed since I landed in Delhi. He advised me to call on the Director of Estates and promised to give me an introduction as the incumbent Indrajit Choudhury IAS (West Bengal Cadre) was known to him. Mr Choudhury readily received me and inquired from the office over the intercom as to why no accommodation was provided to me so far. To my surprise, after five minutes, the same Deputy Director who had been flaunting 'no vacancy' statement every time I met him, walked in to inform that a transit accommodation was available at Tagore Road Apartments. My ordeal in the servant quarter at Niti Bagh came to an end within a month. Again I was lucky to get a type III accommodation shortly thereafter and on Dipawali day 1978, I moved into the same where I was destined to complete a major part of my tenure.

While at Tamil Nadu House, often my wife used to walk up to Teen Moorty Circle with the children every evening. I used to walk back from North Block after office hours and meet the family at the assigned point. After spending the evening in the park, we used to walk back to Tamil Nadu House as darkness descended.

One afternoon the kids wanted to undertake the expedition on their own and slipped out of Tamil Nadu House when their mother was going through newspapers in the lounge. After a few minutes, she noticed the absence of the children and rushed out on the road making frantic inquiries at every corner. Finally, she could get concrete information about the direction the children were headed to and requested a cyclist to go ahead and secure them while she would follow. As expected, they were finally located at Teen Moorty and stopped while trying to cross the road. God was extremely kind and saved us from losing our children.

While at Minto Road, the two again set out on an adventure on a Sunday morning. A multi-storeyed building was coming up within the campus and a huge tank for soaking bricks was built. The water was six feet deep. The second son (two plus) slipped into the tank and nearly got drowned. A good Samaritan watching the incident from a nearby flat, rushed in the nick of the moment to save the child.

Two years later, we had planned to go to India Gate Lawns to witness the Republic Day Parade. My wife had washed the woollens the previous day so that they could be used on the occasion. To our great dismay, someone had intruded in the rear balcony where the woollens were being dried in the sun and decamped with all of them. One hardly needs to describe the misery that befell the family in the midst of a severe winter. Damage control involved day and night knitting by my wife, who was able to replenish the stock in a week. The budget did not permit the purchase of readymade woollens.

With two tragedies in the family in quick succession (my father and eldest brother passed away in Patna within a span of three months) about one third of the take home pay had to be diverted for helping the family in crisis. This lead to a virtual showdown with the budget and invariably old newspapers had to be pulled out to see through the last two days of the month.

Incidentally, my first posting in CBI was that of Assistant Inspector General. In other words; I was a staff officer to the Chief. Some of the officers intending to call on the Director used to spend a few minutes in my room before proceeding to room no 114, Chamber of the Director CBI. It was very difficult to entertain them in view of the acute resource crunch. On many occasions, I had to take a long walk back home from North Block to Minto Road since the last pie would have been spent on tea.

One lucky evening, when I had my return fare intact, a stranger accosted me in the queue—"Sir, which is the way to Madras Hotel"? Waiting for bus No 70, Naraina Vihar to Jantar Mantar, I advised him to come along with me. We got down at Jantar Mantar and started walking through Parliament Street towards Connaught Place. My intention was to show him the location of the hotel and push off to Minto Road. Since the stranger wanted to go to Madras Hotel, I wondered if he had any link with Tamil Nadu. He confirmed the same and indicated that he hailed from Tirunelveli. Instantly, I started conversing in Tamil—"Where are you staying in Delhi"? "Meena Bagh MPs flat, sir". "Which MP"? "Vai Gopalswamy, sir". I said I knew him. The stranger was surprised—"*Eppadi, sir*? (how Sir")? "I was SP of that district". He immediately put a brake and had a good look at me before blurting out—"*Yen, Sir—nadanthe poringeh*? (Why are you going by walk, Sir)? It was beyond his imagination that a person of the rank of SP had to walk. I smiled, "This is Delhi. Here even IGs have to travel by bus and walk if required to".

On seeing my plight, one of my junior colleagues from Tamil Nadu who had come to call on me during an official tour to Delhi, instantly formed his reservations on the idea of seeking a deputation to Delhi. He started with a conviction, "*Sir, naan intha oorukke varave maatten*. (Sir, I will never come to this place"). He continued in his jocular style, "When I go back I will tell all our colleagues that I visited Delhi and found our District SP sitting on a foot path with a bedsheet spread in front of him and people throwing coins. I also dropped ten paise. Sir, even if the Director CBI invites me I am not prepared to come here".

More bouts of anxiety awaited me when I took this officer home for dinner. On seeing the telephone at my residence the officer felt encouraged and asked, "Sir, does your telephone have STD facility"? I was thrown into a real dilemma. Private use of telephones was taboo in CBI. In any case there was a stringent ceiling on the telephone bills. I could not straight away work up a lie and give a negative answer, at the same time I wanted to give a negative input. So, I carefully framed my reply, "I tried once, but the STD didn't work". I thought he will get the message that perhaps the facility was not available. This did not discourage him at all and he said, "Sir, I shall try". As he started dialling I commenced praying that it should not work. Surely, my prayers were defeated and in one stroke he got his line through to Madurai and spoke to his better half for about fifteen minutes. This was not enough and he kept the phone informing his wife that he will ring up after half an hour when the children returned home. The incident is narrated to highlight the difference in the approach on subjects relating to financial propriety in a District Official as compared to a CBI officer. Of course, much water has flown down the Ganges since then and attitudes and standards have undergone a drastic change in CBI as well. Austerity is a thing of the past whether it relates to use of vehicles or telephones or any other facility. Reverting back to the episode in a lighter vein, I happened to narrate the same to a priest in Tamil Nadu whose brother was our senior colleague and he also knew this officer referred to in this story. The priest who was also an eminent professor in Economics had a very deep sense of humour. In one of the letters addressed to me he wrote in the last line, "Sir, do you have STD facility in your telephone"?

Another incident requires to be mentioned to highlight the hazards faced by the family although there is no link with the official life. We had a Tanzanian gentleman, John Hungo, as our neighbour. He used to work for All India Radio. His children used to play with our children. The gentleman had pushed off to Vellore with his wife for treatment, leaving his six children to our care. One afternoon, one of the sons had gone to the market nearby. It seems some urchins had teased him with the word 'Habshi' (Negro). He retaliated with his fists. Immediately, a mob gathered and chased him. Seeing the incident from the window my wife pulled the fleeing boy inside and locked the door. Stones were being pelted on our door with the mob demanding the boy to be handed over to them. It was a matter of credit to the lady of the house, who stood firm on giving protection to the boy whose parents were away. She called me on the phone. I contacted Kamla Market Police Station and rushed home. The Delhi police also acted swiftly. By the time I reached home the mob had dispersed after the police had sorted out the matter.

The lady who braved the volley of missiles on the door and gave protection to the boy at great risk to her own life certainly deserved some praise.

My first stint in CBI was as Assistant Inspector General (Policy). It was basically a staff officer's job with a senior staff officer (DIG) as the controlling officer. Usually, new entrants are first posted to investigating units and shifted to Special Units, if the need be, only after sufficient exposure to investigation. At that point of time, I had no specific clue as to why John Lobo thought of a deviation in my case. My DIG informed that the Director felt that the slot should not continue to be vacant when the CBI conference was round the corner.

For a fresher from the district, it was a rather challenging job - organising the conference — selecting the venue, scrutinising the subjects for discussion, preparing notes, listing out reference material, sending invitations, circulating agenda notes to the participants, organising the valediction with medaı presentation and taking care of catering arrangements. Drafting the minutes was one of the difficult tasks as this was the first of its kind undertaken by me and required deep background knowledge of the organisation. Burning midnight oil paid dividends and the conference went off smoothly to the satisfaction of the

Chief. Like all tension ridden events this one also had its own comic relief which was provided by none other than the Chief Guest himself. The entire audience initially got stunned, but later burst into laughter. The Minister of State for Personnel deviated from the draft provided to him and opened his address thus, "What an irony of fate –a person twice rejected for the post of Sub Inspector is invited to give away medals to distinguished police officers". At that point of time, Sanjay and Geeta Chopra murder case involving the dreaded criminals Billa and Ranga was a hot topic. The Chief Guest surprised everybody by stating that he was personally scared of going for morning walks. The oddity of the occasion on which such a statement was made sounded quite jarring.

One of the functions of the AIG (Policy) was drafting citations for the award of medals. One such batch of citations was processed and accepted during the tenure of the Government. The awardees had naturally highlighted in their draft citations, the achievements in the investigation of cases concerning political leaders of the previous ruling party (Congress) and bureaucrats closely linked to them. By the time the medal presentation could be organised the previous Government had returned to power.

The medals for distinguished services were to be presented during the inauguration ceremony of the CBI and State Anti-Corruption Bureaux joint conference and those relating to meritorious services earmarked for the valediction. The distinguished services medals were scheduled to be awarded by the Prime Minister Indira Gandhi and the second category to be given away by the Home Minister Gyani Zail Singh. During the investiture ceremony on the inaugural day someone in the Government took serious exception to some officers being decorated for investigation concerning the VIPs of the day. Actually the presentation ceremony had passed off smoothly. The trouble started during the coffee break after the presentation. One of the awardees attempted to shake hands with an important bureaucrat in the PMO, who immediately recognised him as the person who investigated (the bureaucrat's) case. Instead of extending his hand the bureaucrat flared up and left in a huff. Not many of the invitees noticed this unsavoury incident and the house reassembled for the business session. Hardly had the session proceeded for fifteen minutes when a slip of paper was passed on to the Director CBI who was conducting the proceedings. He handed over the session to the senior most Joint Director and left the venue in a hurry. Most likely the message was from the PMO. He was held up virtually for the entire part of the session on the first day of the conference.

We were told that there was a serious problem with the medals being given to *persona-non-grata* as far as the Government of the day was concerned. Instructions were perhaps issued to scrutinise the citations deeply and explore the possibility of recalling the medals. The investiture scheduled on the valedictory day was postponed indefinitely and an exercise taken up to review the awards already given. This exercise was going in the North Block office of the Director CBI till late in the evening and the citations had to be retrieved from the bundle of files stacked in the almirah of the AIG Policy. The then incumbent who had succeeded me was having difficulty in locating the citations in question. Thus my services were called for since these citations had been drafted during my tenure. At about 8 pm a vehicle picked me up from my residence. The medals for meritorious service were withheld for some time and later handed over personally to the awardees. Those officers, who had received the medals (distinguished service) during the inaugural ceremony, had to suffer more severe ignominy. They had to go back without attending the dinner hosted by the Home Minister to which they were invited as special guests and had turned up in immaculate ceremonial dress (white and white).

My job as ex-officio security officer of CBI took me on night rounds, which gave me an opportunity to detect and expose lapses on the part of various officials with respect to maintenance of physical security and more importantly

-document security. During the night rounds I used to scout for classified documents strewn over the place. One of the documents which I picked up from the corridors of the Head Office at Sardar Patel Bhavan was marked secret and related to a case of hijacking of an Indian airlines aircraft. One can imagine the annoyance of the Director when it was brought to his notice. Similarly, once I noticed a carbon paper left on a typewriter. The mirror image of the paper clearly revealed the contents, which were of classified nature. It was very embarrassing to receive often, half burnt documents retrieved by the Intelligence Bureau from the centralised incinerator located behind the North Block. These documents were sent for destruction in a loose manner although there were clear instructions for the mode and manner of disposal. Although it was difficult to identify the individuals behind such lapses, my stint as Departmental Security Officer gave me an opportunity to sensitise other officers on the need to ensure departmental security.

I look back with great satisfaction on a specific task assigned by John Lobo. The pendency of court cases was a headache those days also. In 1978, about 1600 CBI cases were pending in various courts throughout the country. In fact, addition of new cases was grossly outnumbering the disposal every year. Concerned with the rising trend, the Director desired an indepth study as regards the cause for delay in the disposal of these cases. He identified twelve specific cases for the study. I divided the analysis in two parts. The first part was devoted to tracking the progress of these cases for which I took resort to a graphical presentation. Time elapsed after filing of chargesheet in a particular case was plotted on the X-axis. The numerical strength of witnesses examined on each date of hearing was plotted on the Y-axis. A case with good progress should have shown a high gradient. Unfortunately, this was not the situation with most of the cases and it was exasperating to note that in one particular case (regular case number/2/56 of Delhi branch) the graph showed a perfect horizontal line. In other words, not a single witness had been examined in the past 22 years.

For the other part of the study, I prepared a tabular chart to indicate the proportion of time consumed by stay orders, prosecution witnesses not turning up, defence seeking adjournment, magistrate not appointed, adjournment sought by prosecution, court on leave, etc. The study indicated that on an average, 80 per cent of the delay was on account of stay orders. The Director was quite impressed with the mathematical projection. However, in spite of initiating steps, which are within the control of CBI, the pendency seems to be mounting, causing serious concern to all the players in the criminal justice system. It had crossed the 5000 mark by 1995. The corresponding figures as of today should be anybody's guess and mind-boggling.

Eventful two years and more as AIG (Policy) fetched me two additional responsibilities—First as a Secretary of the Yardstick Committee, headed by JS Bawa, Joint Director (later took over as Director and enjoyed a long stint), and Secondly, as a Secretary of the CBI Manual Revision Committee, chaired by VR Laxminarayanan, a CBI veteran who returned to the state after seventeen years and ultimately commanded the TN Police.

The first committee was required to prescribe the workload of investigating officers in terms of the number of cases they were required to handle in a year. This required collection of enormous data from various branches regarding the time consumed in the investigation of various cases, spread over a particular period. The two AIGs, the other one being PC Srivastava manning the economic offences wing, had to slog quite a bit to collect and collate the required information. Yardsticks were worked out for prosecutors also.

The Manual Revision Committee could not complete its task although lot of spadework had been done. The Chairman got repatriated following a change in the Government and later one of the DIGs AK Banerjee was deputed exclusively to complete the task of revising the manual. The manual was further revised in 2005, and as Additional Director I had the opportunity to edit the same.

After my stint as AIG I got a shift to a central investigating unit. These units had all India jurisdictions and could register cases only with the approval of the Director CBI. At the time of my taking over there were cases referred by the Government of Manipur, pending investigation. These related to allegations of corruption in large-scale purchase of earth rammers, bathtubs, diesel generating sets etc. One case related to land acquisition. These cases involved senior bureaucrats like the Chief Engineer PWD and the Commissioner PWD and were referred to CBI during the President's rule. Conviction was upheld by the Apex Court in the case State vs Awati Ao. The latter was an IAS officer. In this case, he happened to be a party to a conspiracy in giving the contract for purchasing of earth rammers to Sarat Chandra Sharma (whose earlier firm had been black-listed) and that too at an exorbitant rate. Though the accused denied knowledge about the fact of black-listing such denial was proved baseless as he himself had communicated the decision of the Government to the Chief Engineer which was six months prior to the award of contract to another firm of the supplier. Further, the Supreme Court found no extraneous circumstances warranting a lenient punishment.

Investigation of these cases took our team to Imphal where we had to camp for about ten days at a stretch. Our movement, especially to Morey at the Burmese border was fraught with danger in view of the insurgency prevailing there. We had the privilege of visiting the National Memorial at Moirang en route where our National flag was hoisted for the first time on our soil. It was a thrilling experience to have a look at the proclamation of the Indian National Government and also the personal accoutrement of one of the greatest sons of our nation – Netaji Subhash Chandra Bose.

Another set of cases under investigation pertained to diversion and misappropriation of funds provided by the University Grants Commission to some private colleges. Evaluation of the civil works proved to be the cause for delay. Another handicap was the preoccupation of the investigating officers NL Ramnathan and Raghotaman in sensitive cases being investigated by the Special Investigation Cell.

During my stay of over three years in this branch some interesting cases were registered. In spite of shortage of IOs investigation of all these cases was taken up with equal zeal. Some of them had a disheartening end while others gave enormous satisfaction when they got detected and successfully pursued in the court.

Once more there was President's rule in Manipur. Two cases were referred to CBI during this period. The allegations related to misappropriation of essential commodities. The state was allocated a quota of RBD (Refined Brominated Deodorised) palm oil to be imported and utilised for public distribution. The oil was to be imported by the State Trading Corporation and handed over to the authorised agents of the state governments concerned. Calcutta was the port of entry from where the agents had to lift the stock and transport it to the states concerned for public distribution. Raids conducted by the Enforcement Wing of Calcutta Police revealed that substantial part of the stock had found way to the local market for open sale. Thus, there was large-scale diversion of the oil intended for public distribution in Manipur. Apparently, the Government Officials were in league with the accredited agents.

Investigation began in the right earnest and voluminous documents were collected from the Government of Manipur. However, shortly after the commencement of the investigation, President's rule was revoked and a popular government sworn in. The FIR reflected names of important persons of the popular government including the concerned minister Hthang Jom. After we sent replies to some queries raised by the government of India about the progress of the investigation there was a sudden development in the case. The state government withdrew the consent under Section 6 of the Delhi Special Police Establishment Act 1946; thereby denying any legal authority to CBI to investigate cases in Manipur. CBI was left with no other option but to file closure report in the court. Indeed a frustrating experience. It appears that the withdrawal of consent was prompted by the rapid progress of investigation which would have embarrassed the VIPs. The investigating agency had to pocket the hit below the belt due to legal constraints. Much later courts have ruled that sanction once given cannot be withdrawn.

One case, where no stone was left unturned yet success eluded us, was the murder of Mustafa Al Marzook, a Kuwaiti diplomat at Geetanjali Enclave, South Delhi. Two Palestinian youths were suspected in this case. They fired at the diplomat indiscriminately when he was taking out his car from the garage on 2.6.82 and escaped in a taxi. The taxi number was flashed over the police network and the alert policemen intercepted it at South Extension. Satvir, the cab driver, identified two Palestinian students from the album of photographs of Arab students taken by Delhi Police during demonstrations.

Delhi Police identified the two suspects as Ibrahim and Abdul Jalil. Both had Jordanian passports and were studying engineering at Kurukshetra; located in Haryana. Immigration records revealed that both had crossed over to Pakistan at Wagah border in Punjab on 31.5.82.

The case was transferred to CBI by Delhi Police on 2.8.82. It was earmarked to my branch where AK Suri, DySP was the IO. I had to supervise the investigation and had to report the progress to my DIG R Sekhar, an outstanding officer, who later headed the organisation. Our first venture was to Kurukshetra where the suspects were staying in their hostel rooms, but the same were found locked. The locks were broken and the rooms searched. It was obvious that both had decamped. They had torn into tiny pieces many photographs and letters. These bits of papers and photographs were taken to Delhi and meticulously pieced together to reconstruct them.

The reconstructed photographs threw light on the fellow students of the two suspects. The letters also led to other Palestinian students staying in rented accommodation in Delhi. The gigantic efforts made to piece together the remnants of an inland letter paid rich dividends. The originating address led us to a rented accommodation in South Delhi. The house was owned by a retired army major who was himself residing on the ground floor. From his records it was gathered that Ibrahim had stayed there till July 82, thereby throwing up the possibility that the suspect duo could have travelled back from Pakistan clandestinely after crossing the Wagah border on 31.5.82.

Hence, we started looking for the two suspects without whose examination we were not in a position to think of any other line of investigation. Along with AK Suri I kept on burning mid-night oil working on the motive angle. Following the Delhi incident there were murderous attacks on Arab diplomats, those belonging to United Arab Emirates at Bombay and Karachi where the assailants could escape. However, a young Palestinian who stormed the United Arab Emirates embassy in Kuwait and fired on the Ambassador without success was overpowered and jailed for 25 years.

The series of attacks indicated a common motive on the part of a Palestinian group. Intelligence inputs revealed this group to be that of the dreaded terrorist Abu Nidal. Perhaps they felt that the affluent Arab states like Kuwait and UAE had not done enough for the Palestinian cause.

The factual details of the various incidents were studied and certain common features identified. Investigation took me to Kuwait where the authorities were extremely cooperative in facilitating the interrogation of the accused in the case relating to the attempt to murder the UAE diplomat. The accused was a smart young Palestinian with a background in engineering studies and very proud of his deed. All that I could elicit from him was that he belonged to a very committed group where no member could question the high command on any task assigned and that the left hand was not supposed to know what the right hand was doing. Hence, no information could be obtained about the link between this person and the suspect in our case or about their common goal. Nevertheless, based on the identification by the taxi driver Satvir and their suspicious conduct Ibrahim and Abdul Jalil continued to be the prime suspects. Satvir was placed before an expert who could draw sketches based on the description provided by a witness. The sketches also matched with the photographs of the suspects.

Our pursuit of these persons took us to Aligarh Muslim University where many of their friends were enrolled as students. Three of us – AK Suri, RS Dhankar and I proceeded to Aligarh by the morning train (Assam Mail) and checked in at the University Guest House. After the days work, when we were about to retire, a message came from the city SP that we should contact him at once. It was eleven in the night. The SP mentioned about a call from our DIG R Sekhar.When we rang him up he asked us to rush back to Delhi instantly to follow up an important lead.

I requested the city SP to arrange a taxi. He in turn asked the local Inspector. After about an hour the Inspector turned up with an old ambassador driven by a young person and put us in. As soon as the Inspector went out of sight, the driver started grumbling that after a whole day's work he was back just an hour ago and had no sleep. He was pleading to be excused. We cajoled and convinced him that we shall be alert.

What happened thereafter was a nightmare. Hardly had we moved out of Aligarh, the heavy arrears of sleep weighing on the eyelids of the driver started pulling us towards our end. At frequent intervals, he would lose his bearing involuntarily and the car would swerve towards the ditch on the left. Immediately, a chorus will go up and the driver would just manage to put the brakes. This went on till we reached Khurja about 40 kilometers from Aligarh.

I ordered the driver to stop at a dhaba so that all of us could have some tea and drive away the sleep. By the time

I could finish my cup of tea the driver had hit one of the cots laid on the roadside and started snoring. With great difficulty we could wake him up and force him to take the wheels again.

The same antics resumed within ten minutes and I could not bear it anymore. I got into the driver's seat and pushed him aside. He was only too grateful and instantly fell asleep. I had not driven any vehicle for the last four years and normally would not have dared to drive on the Grand Trunk Road, that too at 4 am in the morning, against the steady stream of dazzling lights of vehicles whizzing past. Perhaps the call of duty provided the impetus and the requisite courage. By the time we reached Ghaziabad, it was daybreak and the driver got up refreshed. He volunteered to complete the rest of the journey.

The raid for which we were asked to rush up had already been completed with the help of some other team, but when we reached office, assignments were already waiting to be followed up. The help of Interpol was sought to locate Ibrahim and Abdul Jalil. I left CBI on completion of my tenure and returned to the state by the end of 1983. My successor in CBI pursued the case, but finally the same had to be closed as CBI could not secure the suspects and extradite them although they were located in Spain.

A puzzle entrusted to my unit was a case referred by the Food Corporation of India. For centralised purchase of fumigation covers the FCI had floated a tender. The material was required to cover the grains after fumigation so that the disinfectant (methyl chloride) could not escape. The vendors were required to enclose samples of the material for technical evaluation. These samples were sent to the Central Food Technological Research Institute (CFTRI), Mysore for analysis. In response, FCI received two reports from the laboratory with contradictory findings. While one report showed company 'A' as failed and 'B' having passed, the other reported the opposite conclusions. FCI sought clarification from CFTRI. The latter confirmed the report showing 'A' having failed as genuine and the other report as fake. FCI referred the matter to CBI for investigation.

Investigation took me and the investigating officer SB Sinha to CFTRI. A slip of paper containing some telephone numbers written with pencil and recovered from the table of a steno gave us the necessary lead. These numbers were traced to be of the owner of company 'A'. Systematic interrogation of these people revealed that a stenographer working at the lab had been bribed by company 'A' to type out the fake report by reversing the findings of the genuine report. However, he had not cared to withhold the genuine report, and by mistake, sent both the covers, containing the genuine and fake reports respectively, to the despatch section. The rest of the job consisted of formalities only.

A detection worth recalling relates to a case of organised fraud which had its hub in the office of the Director General of Technical Development (DGTD). A firm of Bangalore styled as M/s Fritz Godfrey had approached the Steel Authority of India for allotment of steel it required to fabricate a factory, which would be producing metal oxide film resistors. Along with this correspondence was enclosed a photocopy of the registration certificate purportedly issued by the DGTD, New Delhi to the firm. The SAIL requested the firm to transmit a copy of its income tax clearance certificate. The letter was returned undelivered since the postal address furnished by Fritz Godfrey was fictitious. SAIL smelt a rat and referred the matter to DGTD. The latter verified from its records and concluded that the registration certificate was bogus and sought the services of the premier Investigating Agency to solve the puzzle. The investigation was entrusted to our branch.

Since Fritz Godfrey was a non-existent firm, we had to proceed with the probe on trial and error basis. Scrutiny in the office of SAIL, Bangalore revealed that there were six more applications from other non-existent firms. Thus, the possibility of an organised racket became quite clear. While perusing these and other files at DGTD we tumbled upon an interesting feature. The covering letter of a non-existing firm M/s PDJ and Sons enclosing its application was typed on the same typewriter, which was used for preparing a note in the notesheet portion of the concerned file. Following this clue the concerned dealing assistant in the office of DGTD was interrogated along with the typist at length. They disclosed that one peon used to visit them and get applications of the parties typed. The peon was called and he in turn took us to the public relations counter clerk in DGTD who appeared to be the mastermind behind the racket and was in league with the beneficiaries who, incidentally, all hailed from Bangalore.

Both the employees revealed that M/s Jyothi Electronic Service, MR Jyothi and one Srinivas Gupta were in touch with the peon referred to and were visiting Delhi often. The latter also visited Bangalore by air along with his family and stayed in hotels at the expense of the parties. The peon revealed that he was supposed to receive a postal remittance of Rs 2000 from the concerned party in Bangalore. Without wasting a minute the investigating officer rushed to the post office and seized the relevant money order form. The sender's address was noted down and the team left by air to Bangalore and swooped upon the person sending the money order. No incriminating documents were found at their premises but sustained interrogation led Mr Gupta to reveal the involvement of one Nisar Ahmed. His house search yielded a number of incriminating documents along with the office copy of the covering letter of Fritz Godfrey, which was the starting point of the investigation. This was the most crucial document to nail the conspiracy.

We further proceeded to apprehend one SK Jain and G Desu Reddy, a law graduate. Search of their premises led to the recovery of a gunny bag full of blank letterhead pads, rubber stamps of various government departments, and service stamps. When we were conducting the operation the master forger was caught in the act of actually practicing the signatures of various government officials.

Investigation established that on the basis of the registration certificates issued by the DGTD the parties used to procure cement release orders from cement controllers at Bangalore, Bombay and Madras and on the strength of these orders and purchase huge quantity of cement and sell the same at premium. Similarly, Fritz Godfrey attempted to obtain steel. The case was charge-sheeted but it is a matter of dismay that the trial is far away from completion even after twenty-five years, thanks to the dilatory tactics of the accused.

Another ingenuous detection was the case relating to the unnatural death of a young woman within a year of her marriage. Usha Nagpal was fairly educated, completing her post graduation in English from Punjab University; Chandigarh. Her marriage was arranged with Satish Nagpal of Faridabad, who passed himself as an engineer, while in reality he was only a commerce graduate working as an accounts clerk in a commercial firm.

This was the first case of dowry death taken up by CBI. The bride was the daughter of Makhan Lal Nagpal, a businessman from Nagrota in Himachal Pradesh and was distantly related to the groom's family. The couple went to Shimla and Dharamsala for honeymoon, but their relationship got strained right from the beginning and Satish left Usha with her parents, never bothering to bring her home. Somehow, her parents managed to leave her at in-law's place.

Usha realised that everything had changed. Her in-laws were taunting her at every opportunity and asking her to write to her brother in USA to bring gold from there. Her life became miserable and under a state of depression she asked the domestic servant Chandramohan to bring Finit (insecticide) and sleeping pills to commit suicide. The servant could not succeed in procuring the same.

One morning, Usha went up in flames in the kitchen. Her in-laws made out a story that this was a case of accidental fire accentuated by a leaky kerosene stove. The accident is said to have occurred when Usha Nagpal was preparing tea. During inquest the local police confirmed this version. What was strange is that the forensic expert held a spot demonstration to show how kerosene would have leaked from the stove. The post-mortem simply indicated that death was due to asphyxia. After the incident, the brother of the deceased, a professor of Chemistry in USA, kept on petitioning to the Government of India for an impartial investigation. The case was ultimately transferred to CBI and our unit got the opportunity to solve the case. The investigating team withstood intense political pressure and rose up to the occasion.

As the first step records were taken over from the local police. A photograph of the scene taken after the accident threw up startling revelations. It depicted the kitchen with the portion of the floor freshly mopped, a kerosene stove kept on one side with a bottle of kerosene near by. After a fire accident there could not have been any possibility of the mopping mark persisting. The same should have dried up instantly due to the heat. Further, there was no symptom of any disturbance. It was obvious the scene was simulated and that too carelessly. No kerosene residue was found on the burnt clothes. Most probably death was due to suicidal hanging.

Usha was not happy with the marriage since she did not enjoy the confidence of her husband. Further, there were indications of mental torture by the family to bring in gold and money from her brother settled in USA.

Examination of witnesses revealed that there was a servant boy Chandramohan working in the family for the past few years. He was relieved shortly after the incident and despatched to his native village in Uttar Kashi. Sensing that he could be a crucial witness; the investigating officer PB Sundriyal immediately sent a team to locate the boy. Usha's in-laws also launched a drive simultaneously. We were lucky to reach the boy first. His interrogation confirmed that Usha's in-laws were pressurising her to bring in gold and cash and ill treating her. He particularly mentioned the role of Satish and his elder brother's wife Surendra.

Charge-sheet was laid against Satish Nagpal, husband, and his brother's wife Surendra Nagpal under Section 306 IPC (abetment to commit suicide) and 120B IPC (criminal conspiracy).

Defence tried their level best to win over the crucial witness Chandramohan, servant boy, but the latter stuck to his guns. Surendra was acquitted, but Satish convicted to three years RI by the Sessions Court, Ambala. However, during the pendency of his appeal before the High Court he expired in a road mishap.

Chapter – 10

Eventful Stay in the Temple City

The first two years at Delhi put us through a tough ordeal, especially for the lady of the house who had to run the household virtually single-handed. With no telephone for the first two years or any transport at home, a cramped accommodation, frequent invasions by visitors of all hue and two personal tragedies to top it, life was rather depressing. However, we slowly started liking Delhi and when my DIG Rajendra Sekhar, later became director CBI, sounded me for an extension of two years I readily agreed. But strange is the way the bureaucrats react to situations. Two years ago, when I wanted to return to the cadre the same was viewed with displeasure and now that I wanted to continue, the mandarins in North Block insisted that the tenure rules be applied strictly. The discrimination was sickening. I know people who have continued on deputation for twelve years at a stretch, when I approached the Director JS Bawa he reacted coolly and said that he would be taking up the matter with the Government once only and beyond that he was helpless. Needless to mention, his first attempt itself resulted in failure, as it was a mere formality.

I was relieved in the first week of November, 1983 after a stint of five and half years and returned to Tamil

Nadu at great inconvenience to the children, who were half way through the academic session. Although informed in advance about my repatriation, the DGP refused to propose any posting till I reported Madras. In fact, when I met him during his camp Delhi he was visibly annoyed to learn about my repatriation. Perhaps he was under pressure from my juniors to block my return lest it spoils their promotion chances. It was very difficult to convince him that it was not my decision. So, here was a situation where one felt unwanted in both the places.

I reached Madras on the 8th of November, 1983 to face a phenomenon first time in my career—'compulsory wait'. I learnt that it was the order of the day. I was also told that I was lucky as my wait ended in just 20 days. There were others who had to cool their heels as long as 60 days or more.

Since I had already seen two district postings I requested the IG, Law and Order and the DGP a placement in Madras. The request went unheeded and I landed up in Madurai to take over as SP Madurai North.

This happened to be the longest field posting for me, nearly three years and of course, a very eventful one.

Madurai had a compliment of six IPS officers—namely, the DIG Madurai range, Superintendents of Police Madurai City, Madurai North (later named as Madurai Rural after formation of Dindigul District), Ramnad East, Ramnad West and Civil Supplies CID. The SPs functioned from their isolated posts with very little interaction at social level. Taking advantage of my seniority I initiated steps for forging a warmer relationship. At regular intervals, we started gathering at some SP's residence after the day's work. Potluck dinners used to be arranged, followed by film shows (video screening). A doctor from Bombay, engaged by the district administration for the family planning programme, used to lend video cassettes of English classics. Sometimes we used to go for night shows in the theatres. Soon, the Collector also joined the bandwagon.

When there is requirement of additional force from another district within the same range the approval of the DIG is required. The same applies to the services of an SP required in another district. To meet emergent situations, we cut short the process and evolved a system of helping each other *suo-motu*. One evening, SP Ramnad West, Ramanujam, informed me that Nagamalai Pudukottai station is being attacked and SP Madurai City RN Sawani was facing the mob. Instantly, we left with a striking force and assisted SP City in restoring normalcy. Similarly, I decided to rush to Dindigul on my own to assist SP Dindigul S Ramanathan when violence in a political party procession led to police firing.

When the Chief Minister Dr MG Ramachandran was to visit Kodaikanal along with Mother Teresa and Farooq Abdullah, CM of Kashmir for inaugurating the Mother Teresa Women's University and renaming the Kohinoor Bungalow as Sheikh Abdullah Maligai, we established perfect coordination amongst ourselves with Ramanujam looking after the public meeting at Batlagundu, KVS Gopalakrishnan, SP City, incharge of the airport and convoy and myself at the helm at Kodaikanal. The DIG was to accompany the VVIPs. It was apprehended that he would pick holes in the arrangements en route. So, a small conspiracy was hatched to escape from the running commentary over the VHF network. In the tension of receiving the CM at the airport the DIG failed to notice that the city SP had put him on board a vehicle which was not fitted with a mike (VHF). We had absolute peace over the network for the entire three hours period the convoy took to reach Kodaikanal.

Although Tirunelveli was rated as a problematic district with frequent caste flare ups and a highly polarised constabulary to boot, my tenure, though a short one, passed off without any caste or communal murder, any death in custody or police firing. Comparatively, Madurai North proved to be a treasury of unpleasant incidents. To quote a few, the one which comes to mind first is the clash at Gudalur (Cumbum) involving Gounders and Thevars.

It was 11th of September, 1985. I had invited a few guests on the eve of my son's birthday. Leaving the arrangements in the hands of my wife I had to rush to Gudalur, a good three hours drive from Madurai, to sort out the issue. The whole problem started with the death (natural) of a Gounder. As per the prevailing custom, the body was to be washed with well water. Traditionally, water from a well belonging to a Thevar was used. The Thevars put up a strong resistance and in fact, closed the well by dumping debris. Though there was some retaliation by the Gounders, Thevars were clearly the aggressors and indulged in large-scale vandalism, arson and looting. When I reached the place, a petrol pump belonging to a Gounder was being attempted to be set on fire and traffic was paralysed. One Gounder was killed in the clashes.

After stationing armed police at sensitive points and arranging mobile patrols we tried to bring about reconciliation between the two castes, but in vain. Vandalism stopped in the town, but spread to the agricultural farms nearby. The Gounders were the owners and the labour largely comprised of Thevar community.

For the next three days, I parked myself in the police station. Often war cries will be heard in the night and we would have to stand between the two factions and chase them away. The third day traffic was resumed. Search teams were organised, who started effecting arrest and recovery of looted property. Motor pump sets were the common target. The Chief Minister had programmed a four-day visit to the district. He was to arrive at Madurai on the 14th of September, inaugurate Anna district (Dindigul) on the 15th, attend medal parade the next day at Madurai and address a public meeting at Andipatty, his constituency, on the 17th of September.

After Gudalur started limping back to normalcy, I started for Andipatty on the 14th morning to inspect the arrangements for the impending public meeting. There I met the DIG, GS Ramanan. After the inspection, the latter insisted that I returned to Madurai to receive the CM. He pointed out that it was Madurai North district from which Anna (Dindigul) district was being formed and propriety demanded that the SP of the mother district be present. I promised to proceed to Madurai after completing the briefing at Andipatti. The DIG left but I could not proceed to Madurai.

Information was received that there was a death in custody in Thevaram police station and the body was still there. I promptly started for Thevaram. A young boy Dhanuskodi of Dalit community was brought by the SI Crime from the nearby settlement for interrogation in a theft case. After putting him in the lock-up the SI left. The suspect entered the bathroom, shredded his underwear to make a cord and hung himself from the ventilator. The SI, law and order, committed the mistake of not removing the body immediately, thereby allowing the mob to collect. We tried to convince the leaders that a magisterial enquiry had been ordered and that action will be taken as per his report. Pending the inquiry the SI had been placed under suspension. All arguments fell on deaf ears and ultimately the police station was attacked. We had to open fire (only buckshots) to disperse the mob. Two persons were injured. By that time the RDO had completed the inquest. The body was sent to Uthamapalayam under heavy escort for postmortem. En route, stones were pelted on the van. Late in the night, I proceeded to Uthamapalayam and camped there to ensure that there was no problem during the postmortem or burial. To avoid whipping up of passions once again, we decided to call the relatives of the deceased to Uthamapalayam and carry out the burial there itself.

There was no further problem and I thought I could still make it to Dindigul for the inauguration of the new district. Although a new SP was already in position I considered it a moral duty to be present on the occasion and assist the DIG and the SP. The DIG heaved a sigh of relief on seeing me. He was badly in need of assistance as there was utter confusion about the route to be followed by the CM when the massive procession would most likely jam the streets of the small town. The CM was scheduled to use the chopper from Madurai to Dindigul and drive down to the viewing point in front of the North police station. While we were waiting at the helipad, message came that the CM had already left by road. Since the main route was already choked by the procession I suggested to the DIG to use the bye-pass, circle the town and enter through Vedasandur road. My plan worked well and the CM reached the viewing point without any hitch. However, the road behind the rostrum leading to the traveller's bungalow got clogged and the DGP VR Lakshminarayanan got worried about the CM's passage. I assured him that there won't be any problem. I collected the reserve strength, lined them along the route with instructions to push back the crowd to the sidelines as soon as the signal was given. As the CM got into his car I waived at the men. They did the needful and enough space was created for the convoy to pass through.

When the public meeting was under way the DIG confided that he had received instructions to change the escort officer for the return journey. He felt much relieved when I volunteered to take up the assignment. Well past midnight, I reached home, yearning for a good bath before hitting the bed after five days of ordeal.

Although the violence abated in Gudalur, the simmering tension persisted and took months of social engineering to get dissolved. After the CM's visit was over more manpower was made available and we stepped up police action, effecting arrest of scores of accused and recovered sizeable number of looted property. Inspector Mariappan did commendable work to restore normalcy.

Gudalur being the station bordering Kerala, Kumuli in Iddikki district, we had to deal with occasional border disputes. One annual feature was the puja to be performed in Mangaladevi temple. The devotees were from Cumbum – Gudalur area, but the route was through Kerala. The Kerala administration was very touchy about the security arrangements which it insisted was its domain. Every year it required border meeting between the Collectors and SPs of Iddikki and Madurai respectively to ensure that the festival passed off smoothly.

One had to take the border disputes seriously as under the slightest provocation TN registration vehicles will be stoned at Kumuli and the vehicles from Kerala attacked at Gudalur as was the case when a joint team of Tamil Nadu Forest Personnel and Tamil Nadu Special Police manning a border check post opened fire in self-defence to scare away a gang from Kerala, who had crossed over for poaching and visiting an arrack shop on the TN side. Inter-state traffic was paralysed and unruly mobs had gathered at Kumuli and Gudalur respectively. I rushed from Vaigai dam where I was camping and Desmond Netto, SP Iddikki also dashed off to Kumuli. In spite of solemn assurances that action would be taken pursuant to a magisterial inquiry, the mob did not release the traffic and correspondingly Gudalur people blocked the Kumuli bound vehicles. After the day long blockade, the SP Iddikki felt enough was enough and dispersed the mob by ordering a lathi charge. Consequently, traffic was released both ways. The Collector never turned up. A meeting convened by the Labour Secretary at Madurai was more important.

There was another unsavoury incident involving both the states. Prime Minister Rajiv Gandhi accompanied by Sonia Gandhi was scheduled to visit Thekkadi (Kumuli) in the first week of September, 1985. Since trial landing was not successful, it was decided to land at Gudalur and drive upto Kumuli. The Collector, Iddikki arrived at the helipad and expressed a desire to travel with the pilot. Later, we came to know that the Collector had stopped the convoy at an unscheduled spot on the Tamil Nadu side and requested the Prime Minister to walk upto a settlement on the way side which was geographically located in Kerala. He made impromptu security arrangements by requesting the DySP on route *bandobast*. As this was a serious security lapse and breach of protocol the same was brought to the notice of Government of Kerala for appropriate action.

One evening, when I was getting ready for volleyball in the armed reserve grounds the Special Branch Sub Inspector brought bad news that there was a serious problem at Devadanapatti. The police station was under attack and the police had to open fire. I left for Devadanapatti with the striking force. Onlookers thronging the main thoroughfare started moving away on seeing the reinforcement. The police station wore the look of a battle ground with two bodies lying in the campus, a police motorcycle burnt to ashes and the station records completely ransacked. After the orgy of violence, the troubleshooters had run away but curious onlookers stayed on.

The Revenue Divisional Officer was already available and started the inquest. After bolstering the *bandobast* around the station I had to arrange security for the police line huts as well. It was apparent that the day's incident was only a triggering device for the general discontent nurtured by the community against the local police administration.

On 26.3.86 some students of the high school at Devadanapatty had pelted stones on a private bus. The driver had secured one Velmurugan and seven other students and brought them to the police station. The SI Devadanapatty registered a case in this connection. When the enquiry was in progress, some teachers of the school led by Sanjeevi approached the Sub Inspector with a request for not proceeding with the matter and undertook to pay for the damages caused to the bus. Acceding to their request, the Sub Inspector sent the accused students back to the school. Velmurugan was warned by the teachers and handed over to his uncle. He went home and driven by a sense of shame committed suicide by hanging.

As the news of his death spread like wildfire, one Rajendran and other relatives of the deceased collected a mob of over thousand people and stormed the police station with the dead body, alleging that the police were responsible for the death. All explanations and requests by the Sub Inspector for lodging a complaint fell on deaf ears and the mob attacked the station. They also set fire to the village Administrative Office. The police had to open fire in self-defence which claimed the life of one of the rioteers, Nazar. Cases were registered for the suicide and various instances of rioting. The DIG Madurai joined me and we camped there for the night. Next morning S Sripal IG law and order visited the spot. Normalcy had returned by then.

On the investigation side, one case that gave lot of professional satisfaction was the one relating to the unnatural death of a housewife. Her name was Devaki and the incident took place in Kannamalpuram village in Chinnamanur police station limits. Her body was found in the garden well - situated within the compound of the house owned by her husband Mayandi - and it happened to be their residence. They had a son aged four years.

The case was registered under Section 174 CrPC on the report of the husband that his wife had committed suicide by jumping into the well. The local police had treated the case as one of suicide and the crime would not have seen the light of the day but for a petition (anonymous) received by me accusing the husband. When I referred the petition for inquiry the Inspector, Uthamapalayam Circle examined the medical officer, who had conducted the autopsy and altered the case as one of suspicious death. I was not satisfied with the investigation and summoned the Inspector with the case diary. The postmortem revealed a swelling around the neck of the deceased and indicated death to be due to asphyxia. Apparently, it was a case of strangulation and not drowning. The accused confessed the offence and the towel used for strangulation was recovered.

The case was chargesheeted for murder and tried by the Session Judge Madurai. In view of the distance from the district headquarter and keeping the convenience of the witnesses in mind the proceedings were held on camp. The prosecution relied heavily on the child witness, son of the deceased, but the same was not acceptable to the court. The defence sought to explain the swelling around the neck due to a hit on the pipe used to draw the water. The Learned Judge rightly rejected this claim, since in that case the swelling would not have been formed uniformly around the neck. Further, since the well belonged to the accused, applying deductive logic the accused was held guilty in spite of discarding the evidence of the child witness. The case ended in life sentence.

Orderlies, later called security aides, have been a constant source of entertainment everywhere. Madurai was no exception. Once we went to Salem on camp and were just late for dinner. It was 10.30 in the night. To make things easy for those attending on us we thought of having simply bread and butter. We generally preferred Amul butter but made the mistake of mentioning simply 'Amul' to the SB Head Constable instead of saying 'Amul butter'. We kept waiting and waiting. Finally, he turned up with a tin of Amul baby food, sporting a victorious smile as he had succeeded in waking up the provision merchant and making him open the shop at 11 pm.

An IAS officer, Ashok Rastogi, was visiting Madurai and I invited him for dinner. He wanted a pick up from the hotel. Exactly, at 7 pm I deputed a Special Branch head constable to bring Mr Rastogi from the hotel. The head constable shortly returned after picking up an elderly Bengali couple from the same hotel. The thought of Mr Rastogi had vanished from his head the moment he saw the Bengali couple in an odd place like Madurai. His conviction that the couple had to be my relation got cemented when he heard that they also had the surname Mukherjee.

We did not know whether to laugh or cry. The couple initially had wondered at the invitation from an unknown person, but were scared to disregard summon from the Superintendent of Police. On seeing our bewilderment, they realised the mistake. Nevertheless, having brought them, we had to entertain the guests and behave as if everything was normal. In the meanwhile, Mr Rastogi kept howling on the telephone that the vehicle had not turned up. Profusely apologising to him for the delay we had to politely say good bye to the elderly couple and drop them at the hotel.

The stint at Madurai gave me the opportunity to shape two youngsters -Ashok Kumar (1982) and T Rajendran (1983) both of whom turned out to be outstanding officers.

Chapter - 11

A Brush with Militants

In 1975, Ramnad district had been bifurcated into Ramnad East and West Police Districts with both having headquarters at Madurai. In 1984, the revenue district was trifurcated with headquarters at Ramnad, Virudhnagar and Sivagangai respectively. The police districts were reorganised accordingly, thereby requiring the DIG Madurai range to supervise six districts. This led to the carving out of another range and Ramanathapuram Range was created with jurisdiction over the three new districts, old Ramnad district.

Geographically, Madurai would have been the epicentre for the three districts and ideally suited to be the range headquarters.

The DGP made some efforts in this direction, but the political decision was to have the headquarters at Ramnad. During the President's Rule in 1988, the then DGP made one more attempt to shift the headquarters to Madurai, but in vain.

The mantle of the new range fell on me and I took charge on the eve of Independence Day in 1986. The immediate task on hand was to arrange smooth, free and fair bye-elections in Aruppukottai. An elaborate *bandobast* scheme was prepared and manpower pumped in from TSP and other districts. The CM addressed three public meetings. Although the pre-poll period passed off smoothly, an unfortunate incident on the polling day caste a pall of gloom. A mob organised by a group supporting the ruling party candidate invaded the booth in Thumbuchinampatty village, M Reddiapatty police station, with the intention of booth capturing. The contingent of seven policemen was overpowered and the Talayari, village watchman, hacked to death. By the time, the IGP law and order Mr Sripal and I reached the spot the SP Rathinasavapathy was already present. Many rioteers had been arrested, but the polling was stopped with the dead body lying inside the booth. The Chief Electoral Officer also arrived and desired that polling resume as early as possible. Formalities were completed speedily, the body removed for post-mortem, the booth cleaned and polling resumed in record time. It was a clear case of failure on the part of the police picket as well as the striking force. The SP was directed to institute disciplinary proceedings accordingly.

Handling VVIP visits is common to every field officer. I have had my quota as well, attending about a score of such visits. There was only one occasion on which I had to face tense moments. In fact it was a peculiar problem. It was election time with the Tamil Nadu Assembly polls slated in the 4th week of January, 1989. PM Rajiv Gandhi started the campaign from Virudhnagar on 28.12.88. In the subsequent visit on 9.1.89 he was to cover Thondi, Keelakarai, both in Ramnad district and Tirupattur, Sivagangai district, in my jurisdiction. Refuelling of the helicopters was scheduled at Thondi, however, since the programme at Thondi got cancelled in the last moment, the tanker was diverted to the next venue—Keelakarai which was not adequately prepared to put up a stable helipad.

The helipad was located behind the barricades restricting the crowd and facing the dais. Keelakarai being a coastal area, the fully laden tanker could not negotiate the loose sand and got bogged down at the entrance to the helipad. The driver tried to plod on by changing gears and stepping up the gas. The uniformed personnel also chipped in, but the tanker would not budge.

The struggle going on at the helipad was noticed by the VVIP from the dais and to remedy the situation the entire hierarchy of officers including the DGP, BP Rangaswamy, rushed to the helipad. Any delay in refuelling would have a cascading effect on the PM's programme. First we tried to push the tanker forward manually by engaging scores of people. Next, we put wooden planks before the front tyres and asked the driver to accelerate. It was a war like situation. But the VVIP was unruffled. Realising the futility of the exercise going on to remove the tanker, he decided to move on to Madurai for refuelling and proceed with the rest of the programme.

Before boarding the chopper Rajiv Gandhi suddenly looked back and saw me standing alone, wearing the look of a defeated soldier. To my great surprise he took a few steps towards me and extended a handshake, with an electrifying 'Thank You', so warm that it defied Newton's Laws of Cooling and the warmth lingered on. I shall ever remember that magnanimous gesture laced with a sweet smile. No wonder tears rolled down my eyes spontaneously when I heard the stunning news on the night of 21st May, 1991.

A venture of a new type was "Operation tiger" aimed at disarming the Sri Lankan militants staying in a number of camps. The camps in the coastal area of Ramnad district were perhaps the most active in view of its proximity with the island nation. There were ten camps as noted below.

1. Pirappanvalasai (Tamil Elam Liberation Organisation—TELO)
2. Thoppuvalasai (Peoples Liberation Organisation of Tamils—PLOT)
3. Chatramstreet, Mandapam (PLOT—Uma Maheswaran Group)

4. Railway quarters, Mandapam (Tamil Elam Army—TEA)
5. 27, New Street, Rameswaram (LTTE)
6. Antoniarpuram, Rameswaram (Elam Revolutionary Organisation—EROS)
7. Antoniarpuram, Rameswaram (TELO)
8. Vilunditeertham, Rameswaram (TELO)
9. Nalupanai (Elam Peoples Revolution Liberation Front—EPRLF)
10. Pirappanvalasai (EPRLF)

In view of the large area to be covered, a team from Sivagangai led by SP Chidambaramswamy was summoned to assist the SP Ramnad. I monitored the operation from Mandapam. While there were recoveries from all the camps, the recovery from TELO and EPRLF camps at Pirappanvalasai was mind-boggling. The cache was so huge that it required five lorries to transport it to Madras. There were arms and ammunition of all kinds including rocket launchers with thermal triggering device.

Although the number of weapons was not significant the quantity of ammunition was huge. The total recovery of AK-47 rounds alone exceeded 70 thousand followed by LMG rounds 6150, MMG rounds about 42 thousand, HMG rounds 17695, grenades 1628, two-inch mortar 880,83 mm rockets 220,90 mm rockets 17 boxes, 5.56 rounds 3500 and .25 rounds 4000. The major weapons found were AK-47—6,303 rifle—6 and machinegun-1. Explosives like gun-powder and zeebo explosives were also found in substantial quantity.

The disarming operation was carried out with extreme tact. If there was any resistance from the militants the policemen could have been in trouble. Another potential risk was the possibility of the cadres committing suicide which we realised only on seeing the cyanide capsules hanging around their neck. Although the operation was launched in other districts also, the recovery at Pirappanvalasai was perhaps the largest. The seized articles were deposited at the TSP stores Avadi and are still available.

One gory incident that would keep haunting us was the mass killing that took place in Abiraman police station limits near Mudukulattur. A public transport corporation bus was waylaid and eight persons from Keelakodumalur village hacked to death. One Muthu, an affluent Dalit, who happened to be the Panchayat president of Keelakodumalur village, was brutally murdered by eight of his relatives on 15.2.88 as he had deprived them of their tenancy by purchasing the land from the landlords. An immediate backlash was prevented by the police.

In spite of opposition by the police, who relied on the possibility of a reprisal, the Sessions Court granted bail to the accused within two months and subsequently permitted them to enter Ramnad district with the stipulation that they should appear at Mudukulattur police station every Wednesday and Saturday.

The relatives of the slain president were seething with revenge and chalked out a plan to bump off the accused by storming the bus they were travelling in to visit Mudukulattur. The plan was executed on 16.7.88. Around 0730 hours, 27 relatives of the deceased waylaid the bus at a desolate spot in Abiraman police station limits, threatened the driver and the conductor at gun point, terrorised the other passengers by opening fire in the air and forced them to flee. The targeted people facilitated the attack by simply ducking under the seats without offering any resistance although they were accompanied by four persons armed with sickles. The assailants carried out their job with lightning speed and escaped thinking that all the twelve were dead. One of the victims was able to inflict a spear injury on one of the assailants.

Postmortem was held at Ramnathapuram, 50 kilometres away, instead of neighbouring Mudukulattur in view of the sensitivity of the place. For the same reason burial was arranged at Ramnad, but the relatives of the deceased were adamant to bring the bodies to the village. As sentiments prevailed, the pits dug up at Ramnad were closed after burying a cock (after culling) in each pit. This was to ensure that no bodies arrived at Ramnad.

During the burial at Keelakodumalur village more than 1000 people gathered and in the midst of emotional scenes the eight widows took a vow to leave their hair undressed and not to remove their thali (sacred necklace) till the killers were eliminated. It is to the credit of the police that their vow remains unfulfilled till today. All the 27 accused including three lawyers, one of them got selected as district munsif, were arrested, the tractor used for travel and the weapons seized. The case was built on solid evidence of the four injured eye witnesses who had accompanied the deceased.

However, all expectations of an exemplary conviction stood belied in the additional session's court, Ramnad. The latter accepted the proposition of the defence that the scene of crime was changed by the police and went to the extent of discarding the evidence of four survivors and the bus crew. To comprehend the doubt created by the defence in the mind of the court one has to go through the dynamics of the public transport used by the deceased.

Actual SOC as per investigation (Scene of Crime) The arrows indicate the movement of public transport

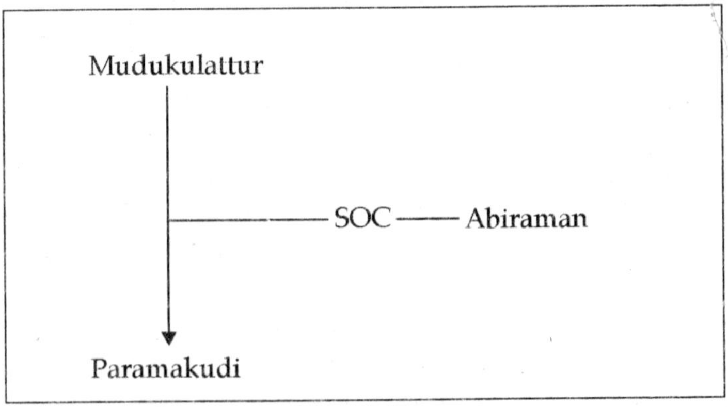

Concocted SOC Advanced by the Defence Lawyer

The bus used to come from Abiraman, visit Mudukulattur and from there proceed to Paramakudi. Hence, it should

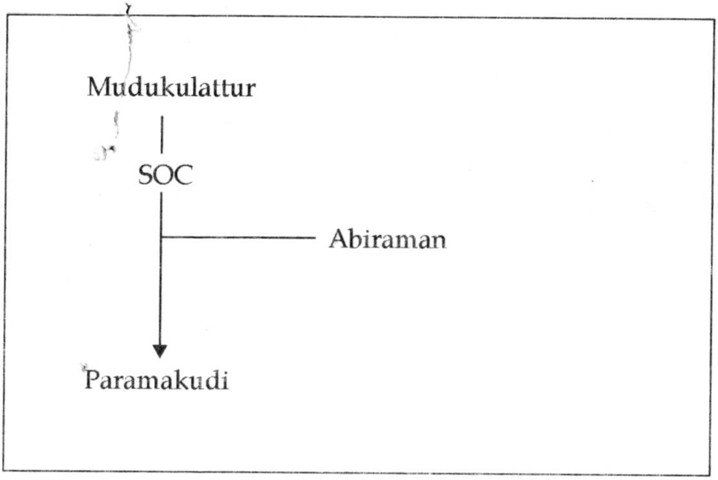

have carried the destination board of Mudukulattur if the scene of crime was as per the police investigation. However, the board depicting Paramakudi as destination was put in at Abiraman itself as it was difficult to change the name board at Mudukulattur bus stand where the crowd would rush to occupy every inch in the bus as well as the roof top. This fact was clearly deposed by the driver and the conductor. However, the court disbelieved the evidence and accepted the suggestion of the defence that the scene of crime should have been between Mudukulattur and Paramakudi. The acquittal filled with gloom the heart of every policeman, who handled this case. With the faint hope of reversing the decision of the trial court and ensuring justice for the deceased an appeal was filed in the High Court on 5.4.91. It took the case nine long years to be disposed off. It was a fit case to be taken to the Supreme Court, but the officers then in command, defaulted. The contradiction between the statements of PW1 and other injured persons whether they went to the hospital together or alone could have been ignored and more importance attached to their version regarding the actual attack.

Even after 17 years of exposure to violent incidents of all type it was very difficult to absorb the tension and maintain composure in this case as it happened. The picture at the scene of crime was too ghastly for anyone to bear—bodies strewn all over and the floor of the bus splattered with blood.

It was pleasing to note that the SP Virudhnagar T Rajendran had rushed to the scene on his own to assist the SP Ramnad K Radhakrishnan, who had already mobilised the force to deal with the grim situation. Luckily, the accused and the deceased belonged to the same community. Nevertheless, we had to strain every nerve to prevent any retaliation.

Chapter – 12

A Date with a Serial Killer

We toiled hard to ensure the smooth conduct of the Assembly elections in 1989. When it was time to relax I had to rush home, Patna, as my mother has passed away. By the time I returned I had already been shifted to Crime Branch CID.

Work here was somewhat like CBI – concentrating on the investigation of the cases entrusted by the courts, the Government or the DGP, organised crime and politically sensitive cases formed the major work load. Cases where the local police could not do justice were also referred to CB, CID. Of course, till that time corruption cases were not entrusted to it and these remained the exclusive domain of the Directorate of Vigilance and Anti-corruption. One wonders whether it was a wise decision to deviate from this tradition later. CB, CID had no expertise in the investigation of cases under the Prevention of Corruption Act. Further, the move gave rise to overlapping jurisdiction concerning the two investigating agencies.

The most memorable case for me was the daring escape of the serial killer, Auto Shankar and his accomplices from the Madras Central Prison. Before narrating this case it is worthwhile describing the serial killing for which Shankar was imprisoned.

Auto Shankar earned the name by virtue of his initial livelihood as an auto driver. His forays into the arrack and flesh trade paved the way for his meteoric rise in the underworld. Of course without the blessings of the custodians of law and order such an achievement was not possible. His nexus with senior police officers became common knowledge and brought shame on the police department. Clients of his flesh trade included senior bureaucrats and politicians. It is this trade which ultimately catapulted him to the world of serial killing.

The associates of Auto Shankar were one Babu, Eldin, brother-in-law, Shivaji, Jayavelu, Selvaraj, Ravi, Rajaram and Sudalai. A prostitute called Lalita was brought from Bangalore by Shankar for his brothel business. He fell in love and married her. He kept her in a portion of a house owned by one Bommiammal at Kalachetra colony. Sudalai was residing in another portion of the same house. He developed intimacy with Lalita and both of them fled, taking cash of Rs 7300 and a camera belonging to Shankar. After making all attempts to trace the duo Shankar lodged a complaint at Tiruvanmiyur police station. The police located Lalita and brought her to the station. As she refused to go back to Shankar the Inspector despatched her to Bangalore in the custody of a police constable. In connivance with the police, Shankar took charge of Lalita en route and brought her back to Tiruvanmiyur. Frustrated over her betrayal, he strangulated her on 28.10.87, assisted by his brother Mohan, Eldin and Shivaji. Shankar removed the jewels he had given to Lalita. The dead body was taken to the liquor godown of Mohan and buried.

Shankar also decided to finish off Sudalai. He took the latter on 28.2.88 in his car to the arrack shop of Mohan and strangulated him with the help of Babu, Eldin and Shivaji after getting him intoxicated. The gold jewels were removed and the body was set on fire. The partially burnt corpse was wrapped in a bed sheet, taken to Muttukadu and thrown in the back waters.

Ravi, one of the associates, started enquiring from Shankar about Lalita and Sudalai and kept on extracting money through blackmail. Hence, Shankar decided to bump him off as well.

On 14.3.88 when Shankar was having liquor with Babu, Mohan, Eldin and Shivaji at Tiruvanmiyur, Ravi came there and joined the party. He demanded an auto from Shankar. The latter and his associates strangled him with a towel. With the help of mistry Thoppai and painter Munuswamy, Babu dug a pit near the bathroom of the said house. After sending the mistry and the painter away the body was buried in the pit. Both for Lalita and Ravi the pits were covered by plastering.

Sampat, Mohan and Govindraj of Mandavali used to visit Tajmahal Hotel in Tiruvanmiyyur from where Shankar was running his brothel trade. On 29.5.88 in the afternoon while coming in an auto they saw Anita, a prostitute. They were in a drunken mood and attempted to molest her. Eldin coming that way intervened, but was beaten up. When the incident was reported to Shankar, he collected his men and attacked Sampat, Mohan and Govindraj. The three were taken to the arrack shop of Mohan and severely beaten with casurina sticks and wooden reapers and lodged in a store room. Sampat and Mohan died and Govindraj was lingering for life. Subsequently, he was finished off by strangulation. A house was under construction in front of the scene of crime. The three bodies were buried in the trenches and covered with sand.

The elder brother of Govindraj lodged a complaint of man missing with Abhiramapuram police station on 31.5.88. The driver of the auto, in which the three deceased had travelled, also preferred a complaint at Tiruvanmiyur police station on which a case of wrongful confinement and assault was registered. Similarly, the mother of deceased

Ravi filed a case at Tiruvanmiyur police station and the same was registered as 'man missing'.

The complaints regarding the abduction and subsequent missing of Sampat, Mohan and Govindraj led to the unearthing of the serial killing. Babu, one of the accused, gave a confession and later turned approver. Accused were arrested and bodies of Lalita, Ravi, Sampat, Mohan and Govindraj were exhumed and identified through superimposition technique. Postmortem indicated death due to sudden violent attack and unnatural in nature due to asphyxia and strangulation.

Further investigation was taken up by CB CID and Inspector Meer Shoukat Ali turned out outstanding work in exposing the overt acts of each accused. Chargesheet was filed against 1. Auto Shankar. 2. Eldin. 3. Shivaji. 4. Jayavelu. 5. Raman alias Rajaraman. 6. Ravi. 7. Palani. 8. Paramasivam. 9. Mohan (Shankar's brother) 10. Selvaraj.

The High Court confirmed the death sentence on Shankar, Eldin and Shivaji and life sentence against Jayavelu, Raman and Ravi while acquitting Palani and Paramasivam. Mohan and Selvaraj were awarded life sentence later as their case was split up since they were absconding. The Supreme Court confirmed the death sentence on Shankar and Eldin, but reduced the punishment of Shivaji to life imprisonment. Shankar and Eldin were hanged in 1995. Mohan was secured at Pune on 25.6.92 and Selvaraj at Bombay on 20.8.93. They were convicted on 25.11.05.

The serial killings orchestrated by Auto Shankar and his gang led to a great sensation and hit the headlines. The detection and conviction of this case was indeed a feather in the cap of CB CID. Little did we know what more commotion was awaiting us? Shankar, his brother Mohan and Selvaraj remanded in this case, escaped from Madras Central prison on the night of 20.08.90 alongwith their cellmates Kumar alias Sundal Kumar and Vakkil Raja, concerned in a murder case of Palur police station and a theft case pertaining to Chintadripet police station. The daring escape became a hot topic and caused serious concern to the Government about the security in the prisons. In the complaint lodged by the prison department, jail wardens Kannan and Balan and assistant jailor Rahim Khan were arraigned as accused along with the escapees. Immediately, after registration of the case by Chennai City Police, it was transferred to Crime Branch CID for further investigation. The Government of Tamil Nadu also set up a commission of inquiry under the chairmanship of Justice MM Ismail.

The escape was a dramatic one. Initially, it was thought that the accused had fled by getting into an empty tanker. However, we knew that the real story could be unearthed only after arresting the accused. With a view to apprehending Auto Shankar, Mohan and Selvaraj, a systematic manhunt was launched on the basis of data available in the case diary pertaining to the serial killing. A chart was prepared listing out the names and addresses of all people with whom the three of them had some contact or the other. The chart contained as many as forty places to be covered. Teams were formed to keep a watch on these places and censorship was resorted to.

As far as Vakkil Raja and Sundal Kumar were concerned, informants were set up and we started tracking their movements. An inland letter recovered during house search of Vakkil Raja came in handy. It led us to an address at Red Hills. Enquiries at this address revealed that the duo had stayed there the previous night and left in the morning. Finally, one Nagappan, maternal uncle of Sundal Kumar provided the vital information about their whereabouts. The information was followed up with utmost speed and a team led by Inspector Periyasamy struck gold by picking up both of them from the house of a relative in the outskirts of Bangalore. Intense and skillful interrogation of the two brought out the entire escape story.

Auto Shankar, Mohan and Selvaraj co-accused in the serial killing case, were kept in one cell. Vakkil Raja and Sundal Kumar involved in unrelated cases were lodged in the same cell. Soon they became friends. Lodged in the same prison was a remand prisoner Venkatesan involved in theft cases. His sister Devi used to visit the Central Prison to meet him. In the process, she developed intimacy with Auto Shankar. His irrepressible passion for her led Shankar to decide on jail break to unite with her. Their contact continued even after Venkatesan was released and the brother-sister duo became a part of the conspiracy. The first step towards freedom was to organise a system for unlocking the cell. The block in question had some unused cells on the first floor. In one of these cells bunches of rusty old keys of various cells were found dumped. With the connivance of the jail officials, the group gained access to these keys and kept trying their luck with each till they hit the jackpot with one of them.

Next on the agenda was to learn opening the lock by manipulating from inside. Mohan had lanky hands which could pass through the grill of the locked door and operate the duplicate key. Having succeeded in the second step, the group meticulously planned the timing of their flight from the cell, coordinating with the brother-sister combination, who would be waiting outside the perimeter wall for aiding the final act. Every evening, the prisoners used to gather before the TV set for watching the "Light and Sound" programme in Tamil (olium olium). The sound from the song sequences was loud enough to drown any noise that could be created by the group while climbing the wall. This was the ideal time for carrying out the operation.

Venkatesan had managed to climb the tree abutting the outer wall and tied a nylon rope around a branch strong enough to bear the weight of an adult human being. The other end of the rope was tied to a lock. This end was thrown over the wall. Under the cover of the TV sound the escapees climbed the rope one by one. They lay still over the wall in prone position till all inmates had gone back to their cells, jail staff had returned to their posts and silence descended on the prison.

Next, the escapees had to don the role of Tarzan. One by one, they swung down with the help of the nylon rope. With the suburban Park Railway Station at a stone's throw, the group could vanish in no time. They took the wrong train and went up to Tambaram, but returned to the same station as their intention was to escape to Andhra Pradesh. As they were in a hurry, they could not wait for the bus and instead travelled by auto to Tiruvotriyur, but on the way they were stopped by the police, who were doing a routine check. They passed themselves as coolies and returned to Waltax Road bus stand from where they proceeded to Nellore. Their next stop was Cudappah form where Vakkil Raja and Sundal Kumar returned to Madras and went to Bangalore.

Rourkela was one of the likely destinations for Auto Shankar. His father was employed there. We knew that with a woman (Devi) accompanying, Shankar could not continue his run for long. As expected, he finally landed up at his father's place after the other escapees peeled off at Bombay. With the help of Orissa police, Auto Shankar and Devi were secured and flown from Calcutta to Madras to avoid any risk. By this time news had spread like wildfire and the airport was flooded with media people and photographers.

From the airport, the two were taken to the Magistrate for remand and later to a press conference, addressed by the DGP. The latter was so keen to hog the limelight that he ordered the accused to be brought straight to his office for a press conference. As per rules they should have been taken to jail straightaway after the remand order. Allowing the accused to be accosted by the media while in judicial custody was also a serious infringement. Who cares? The image of the Government had been retrieved and the DGP managed a pat on his back and that is what matters. The actual operatives, who burnt mid-night oil and slogged day after day for the success of the manhunt were asked to keep away from the press conference, what to think of any commendation. The only relief from this frustration was the constant encouragement received from C Dorairaj, IG Crime, who monitored every development minutely and arranged the logistic support whatever required. I found him distinctly upset by the brazen display of prejudice by the DGP as far as it concerned me.

The Crime Branch juggernaut rolled on completing the arrest of the remaining accused. After painstaking efforts, Mohan and Selvaraj were secured at Pune and Bombay respectively. Auto Shankar being sentenced to death in the serial murder case, his punishment became redundant in this case. Mohan, Selvaraj, Sundal Kumar, Venkatesan, Devi and warden Kannan were convicted on 3.5.2004 and sentenced to six month, rigorous imprisonment. Charge against Vakkil Raja abated as he died during the pendency of the trial. Jail officials Balan and Rahim Khan were acquitted.

This case is an example of outstanding coordination among the members of the mega team and avid follow up of each bit of information. The outstanding work of CB CID earned laurels for the government as the offenders were brought to book in record time. The entire unit stood mobilised and every member rose upto the occasion. Inspectors Senroyperumal, Mohan, Rajadurai, Bhaskaran and Chinnathamby deserve special mention. The cooperation extended by the Orissa police is indeed praiseworthy.

Chapter – 13

A Brief Encounter with Public Sector at Neyveli

Having spent sometime in an assignment with a similar job profile (referring to my tenure in CBI), I found the stint in CB CID in tune with my preference and professionally satisfying. I was really enjoying the work, but unfortunately even before completing two years I had to pack up and proceed to Neyveli for taking charge of the vigilance, set up in Neyveli Lignite Corporation, a public sector undertaking under the Ministry of Coal. The DGP had suggested this deputation without sounding me at all. This caused me great hardship and I had to leave the family for the sake of education of my children, who were at a crucial stage of their high school studies. Prejudices ran so deep that I was relieved within three hours of receipt of the Government order. My crime was that I had conducted an enquiry under instructions from the then IGP, EL Stracy, in a matter concerning the DIG, P Dorai, who later became the DGP.

Nevertheless, like a loyal soldier I took up the assignment in the right earnest. Immediately, on assumption of charge I set out to study the procedure with regard to contracts and purchases and identified the loopholes in the system so that these could be plugged without further delay. Although

NLC was a profit earning organisation, it was apparent that the profit could have reached greater heights had corruption been neutralised or atleast minimised. While pilferage accounted for a minor part of the loss, mega corruption prevailed in high value tenders.

Regarding pilferage it was obvious that there was rampant connivance on the part of the watch and ward staff and the private security guards engaged on contract basis. Even in the engagement of private security there was substantial corruption. Many duty points required three persons, one per shift. The agency would manage with one or two men, extending their duty hours, while charging NLC for three people. The only solution was to bring in an independent security agency like the CISF. The management, especially those in the finance department, was opposed to this idea, dubbing it as costly. Although the overheads would hike the cost, in the long run the extra expenditure would have offset the losses due to pilferage. I had to take up the matter personally with two successive Coal Ministers for induction of CISF. This also helped in enforcing discipline and cutting the man-hours lost. The unruly of the lot, especially the union leaders, used to come out at their sweet will and pleasure to pursue extra-curricular and personal interests. They were hardly available at their work spots. The supervisory staff was not in a position to take them to task. The existing security set up could not enforce the punching in/out discipline at the gate. With the induction of CISF things had improved a lot as I learnt later.

When I tried to focus my attention to high value contracts/purchases, information started pouring in about the kickbacks. However, these inputs could hardly be converted into tangible material for criminal or disciplinary proceedings. In most of the cases, the tender procedure would have been followed. Further, the departmental vigilance set up enjoyed no statutory powers. Hence, one had to depend on the services of the CBI. Source information was passed on to CBI for taking up open inquiries in the form of regular cases or preliminary inquiries. During my tenure, CBI took up three such issues for investigation under the Prevention of Corruption Act, but in the absence of evidence of quid-pro-quo, could not prosecute any of the officials.

Apart from being hamstrung for want of statutory powers, another handicap for the Chief Vigilance Officer was the dual control under which he functioned. The autonomy possible under the single control of the Central Vigilance Commision was much diluted by the Chief Executive of the public sector undertaking being the first point of control. The management suffered from a narrow mind-set and entertained a conviction that vigilance was an impediment to development, contrary to the proven role of vigilance in achieving growth. Consequently, the CVO and his/her set up were treated as an unwelcome appendage thrust upon by the Government. Any attempt to refer a case to CBI drew allergic reaction and preference was spelt out clearly to limit all punitive action within the purview of departmental action.

It is learnt that the same ethos prevail in most of the PSUs. What is most frustrating is the fact that kickbacks flow even from the lowest bidder (L1), but the same escapes probe as the focus is on the sanctity of the tender process. Another area where hardly anything could be done is the phenomenon of cartel formation.

One of the Chairmen R Gupta felt that there was a possibility that in high value contracts the competent authority or the Board was being misled by the note prepared by the concerned division. He wanted vigilance to have a look at such contract files before decision is taken. I convinced him that vigilance should not be a party to the decision-making process, but to assist him I agreed to put up unsigned scrutiny reports pointing out infirmities in the proposed transaction. Thus, he was in a position to raise queries on the basis of these notes and ensure transparency in the deal. Much later, during an official trip to Hong

Kong as Joint Director CBI, I learnt that the Hong Kong Government had a system to associate their anti-corruption agency "Independent Commission Against Corruption" in the decision-making process and that the system was working well to contain corruption. The construction of the new airport on Lantau Island is a good example.

Within the short tenure of twenty months, I was able to convert the hitherto dormant cell into a proactive outfit, leading to registration of domestic inquiries against twenty-four senior executives, Chief Engineer and above, three cases referred to CBI and loopholes plugged in the disposal system as well as the material receipt system where deception was practised on a large-scale by over-recording the weight of the material. As far as the disposal was concerned, a proposal was made to switch over to postal tendering. However, one felt anguished in failing to do anything with regard to over-recording of the earth work consequent on the flooding of the second mines during the monsoon in 1991. Restoring normalcy was the priority for the management and detection of any irregularity could be done only with the help of surprise check which was unwelcome at that point of time.

Chapter - 14

Back to the State

Due to personal problems, I longed to get back to Madras although I found the job in NLC quite challenging. In spite of recommendation by the Ministry of Coal, the Ministry of Home Affairs turned down my request for premature repatriation. However, the change in Government in Tamil Nadu and its decision to recall my services brought relief. Even then, I had to wait a good five months for getting relieved. The desperation reached such a state that I could hardly think of availing joining time. I got relieved at 1200 hours and drove straight to the Directorate of Vigilance and Anti-corruption the same day at 1700 hours to assume charge as its Deputy Director.

Here again, the tenure was very short, just four months. The work was similar to the one exposed to in CBI. The important events witnessed during the period included culmination of a case of disproportionate assets against a DIG, a scam in the purchase of crash tenders for the Fire Services and a mammoth task in preparing printed books to be used for the appeal pending in the Supreme Court in the Corporation Muster Roll case.

The AIADMK Government instituted a Commission of Inquiry to be presided over by Justice S Sivasubramaniam to look into certain complaints, filed against M Karunanidhi, the then Chief Minister and other party functionaries by K Ramamurthy, MP and Tamizharasan MLA. To assist the Commission, I was appointed as IG on promotion. My association with the Directorate of Vigilance and Anti-corruption got revived when I was asked to assume additional charge of the post of Director from CL Ramakrishnan, who superannuated. It was a proud moment to receive the baton from one of the most brilliant officers of the cadre. The additional charge lasted only for forty days after which RK Raghavan took over.

The new assignment was a slow starter as no staff or logistic support was provided. To propose and get the staff and other facilities sanctioned it took three months. We were supposed to examine witnesses, scrutinise relevant documents and submit our report, based on which the Commission would summon the witnesses and conduct its proceedings. However, the investigation got hamstrung as petitions were filed in the High Court challenging the validity of the Commission. Subsequently, the chairman of the Commission himself was impleaded. Hence, the Commission directed the investigating machinery to limit its activity to examining Government officials and documents alone till the petitions were disposed of by the High Court.

The stalemate continued till I got shifted to Planning and Coordination (Technical Services). I had to rest content by submitting an interim report. My successor also could not complete the task. The Government changed in 1996 with DMK returning to power and the IG Crime was placed in additional charge. He submitted a report holding the allegations as not proved and the Commission adopted the same. Findings of the Commission were accepted by the Government of the day and laid in the Assembly. It remained unexplained as to why the Commission did not proceed when there was no stay. The turn of events was expected due to the unusual delay.

One got the feeling that institution of commissions of inquiry involves wastage of time and expenditure, for if ultimately the prima facie commission of a cognizable offence is made out, the same has to be handled by an investigating agency like CBI, V&AC, CB CID or local police. Commissions are more suited to delve into cases of administrative failure or calamities where the role played by the administration needs to be probed.

An event which had nothing to do with my task at the Commission deserves special mention. A massive job of recruitment of Sub Inspectors was taken up by Vaikunth, DGP and Chairman, Tamil Nadu Uniformed Services Recruitment Board. For reasons best known to him, he decided to utilise my services to head the sub-committee for the selection. In view of my commitments with the Commission, Justice Sivasubramanian was initially reluctant to spare my services, but ultimately agreed to the repeated pleas of Vaikunth.

The ten-day long assignment turned out to be a gruelling one. The day started at six in the morning at the Chingleput East district armed reserve grounds, St Thomas Mount with the certificate verification for about two thousand candidates per day, followed by height and chest measurement. The qualified candidates had to undertake the physical efficiency test. Rope climbing was a compulsory event. Jumping and track events followed thereafter. Options were available for both the items – high jump or long jump, 100 metres or 1500 metres. Those who opted for 1500 metres had to really fret it out with the blazing sun beating mercilessly. It was a pitiable sight watching many of the candidates nursing their blisters after the race.

As twilight brought relief for those conducting the field events, the most difficult part of the process commenced for the sub-committee. Scrutiny of the scoring sheets and related documentation began. One eligible candidate declared as failed or one ineligible person getting through would mean vitiation of the entire process. Thanks to the fool-proof procedure chalked out by Vaikunth and the faultless application by the sub-committee members, the selection turned out to be one of the best. Merit remained the sole criterion.

By the time we wound up, it was usually past dinner time. At the end of the first phase, a pleasant surprise awaited me. Vaikunth entrusted me the responsibility of drafting the question paper for the written test. I finished the job at the same night. Only one copy was made and that too in my own hand-writing and handed over to Vaikunth the next morning. Utmost secrecy was maintained and examination conducted the following day without any hitch.

With a deep sense of satisfaction, I completed the special assignment and returned to the Commission.

Chapter - 15

Tryst with Technical Services

The short period, ten months as the IGP, Planning and Coordination, now known as Technical Services, turned out to be unusually eventful. The supervision extended to Police Telecommunications, the Finger Print Bureau and the Computer Wing. In addition, I had to implement the Police Image Project. This was a useful pursuit, but lapsed into oblivion due to lack of monitoring. With a firm belief in its potential as a remedy to the sagging image of the force, I lost no time to revive it when I got the opportunity to head the force.

Although Tamil Nadu was the first to introduce microwave telephone system, the same based on analog technology, had become obsolete and required upgradation to a digital system. The conversion was a Herculean task and its timely completion was possible only due to solid cooperation between the telecom staff and the vendor Bharat Electronics.

With 157 vacancies in the rank of Sub Inspector (technical) the wing was finding it difficult to cope with the increasing work load. There was also some discontentment with the existing staffing pattern. Both these problems were addressed and proposals initiated for fresh recruitment as well as a comprehensive cadre review. I also decided to visit telecom repeater stations to hear the grievances of the field staff. Working conditions were rather discouraging. I wonder how the staff was traversing the long stretch on the hills to reach the Melpet repeater near Tiruvannamalai. The same condition prevailed at Innadu in Villupuram district. However, here the Collector agreed to help in getting the road repaired. Regarding Melpet, an NGO, Sreenivas Trust, offered help at my instance when I took over as DGP. For setting up a repeater at Arankanal, Dindigul district, to cover the shadow areas of Ramnad, Virudhnagar and Sivagangai districts we had to do lot of spade work starting from land transfer (this being a forest land), to laying down an approach road.

The finger print experts had an association, which was quite vociferous in airing their demands. Confirment of uniformed rank was one of the persistent demands. This unit also required a cadre review. This was gone into meticulously and a comprehensive proposal initiated. The same materialised soon.

Computerisation of finger prints was very much on the cards. The Electronics Corporation of India had come out with the equipment 'Anguli'. It had lent a machine to Tamil Nadu Police to conduct trials on the computerisation of finger print slips. As per the understanding, the trial period was to be one year after which the machine would be purchased, if the trials proved successful. Aided by AIG Farooque, I decided to satisfy myself about the efficacy of the system. I was rather disappointed to find out that feeding the computer with data relating to one FP slip took 75 minutes on an average. These slips related to daily arrests. To complete the data bank it would take 15 to 20 years given the rate at which data was being fed in. Further, this system was not capable of detection of a case by matching a chance print lifted at the scene of crime with the available records. In view of the serious infirmities, the machine was obviously not worth. The same opinion was conveyed by the West Bengal Police who had already tried the system, Anguli.

Hence, we started looking for better options. The one produced by the Computer Maintenance Corporation, Hyderabad was inspected. The Finger Print Automated Coding And Tracing System - (FACTS–03) appeared suitable. The feeding time for each slip was only five minutes and chance print detection facility was available. When the comparative features of both the systems were brought to the notice of the DGP Mr Sripal, he sought specific comments of the DGP Crime. The latter, Rajsekharan Nair, visited CMC along with me and endorsed our findings. However, unexpectedly the adoption of 'Anguli' got proposed in the budget announcements. I conveyed this to Mr Nair. Immediately, he sought a meeting with the Home Secretary, PV Rajaraman. In the meeting, Mr Nair asked me to explain the comparative features. Since the 'Anguli' lacked chance print detection facility, the Home Secretary agreed with us about the need for further deliberations and the matter was shelved.

Another controversial decision that I had to contest with full gusto was the move to celebrate the centenary of the first Finger Print Bureau. The DGP was advised by a retired police officer that Tamil Nadu Police should stake its claim as the first Finger Print Bureau on the basis of a loose-leaf showing the attendance of some staff engaged in finger print work in the year 1895. This was conveyed to the Chief Minister, who agreed to hold a gala celebration in 1995, inviting global personalities. The decision was taken even before I took over as IGP, Planning and Coordination. With the common knowledge that the first Finger Print Bureau was established in Calcutta under the then Inspector General of Police Mr Henry to whose name the ten-digit classifications system was attributed, I decided to cross check the claim by going through the literature available on the history of Finger Print Science. AIG Farooque was of great help in locating the publications. All of them indicated Calcutta as the origin.

Finally, along with Farooque I dashed off to Calcutta to verify the records. At the entrance to the Finger Print Bureau a board is prominently displayed, "Welcome to the oldest Finger Print Bureau in the world". The director was shocked to hear about the claim of Tamil Nadu and informed us that plans were already afoot to celebrate the centenary at Calcutta in 1997. Further, we were taken to the museum where the order (1897) setting up the First Finger Print Bureau was one of the important exhibits. Records revealed that the classification system was developed by Inspectors Hemchandra Bose and Fazlul Haque under the supervision of the Inspector General of Police, South Bengal, Mr Henry. Incidentally, Mr Henry had trained two Inspectors of police from Madras. It appears that these Inspectors assisted by some subordinate staff were attending to finger print work at Madras before the first bureau was formally set up at Calcutta.

Convinced by the position as borne by the records I put up a comprehensive note to the DGP and also pointed out that experts from all over the world might take strong exception to the move of Tamil Nadu Police, which could mar the celebrations. The DGP agreed and the preparations were given a quietus.

Chapter - 16

Second Innings in CBI

In 1994, some reorganisation took place in CBI and posts of Zonal Joint Directors were created. Initially, the incumbents were to function from the Head Office at Delhi. In due course the JDs East, West and South had to relocate themselves at Calcutta, Mumbai, and Chennai respectively. The jurisdiction of JD (South) extended to the four southern states, Andhra, Tamil Nadu, Karnataka, Kerala, and the union territories of Pondicherry and Lakshadweep, with Superintendents of Police stationed at Madras, Cochin, Bangalore, Hyderabad and Vizag and DIGs at Madras and Hyderabad respectively.

With my heart and soul ever embedded in CBI, I readily signalled my willingness when the same was called for a second innings. After a short but stormy stint in Planning and Coordination I left for CBI on the 26th of April, 1995. I was accommodated at New Delhi with instructions to establish the Zonal Office at Chennai as early as possible. Since the Zonal Office at Calcutta had already been set up, the Director Vijay Rama Rao instructed me and the JD West to visit Calcutta and have a look at the Zonal Office. Both of us visited Calcutta and ascertained from the JD East the arrangements he had made for shifting the records from Delhi to Calcutta.

First, space was located at Shastri Bhavan, Madras for my office and record room. The next task was to list out the files and pack them serially. The same was completed in record time of just one month. The heap consisted of 101 bundles, neatly packed in gunny bags and meticulously sealed. After consultation with the Chairman, Railway Board, it was decided to utilise half portion of the luggage van of four ton capacity attached to Tamil Nadu Express. The loading was done in my presence and our lock was put on the shutter duly sealed. I decided to travel by the same train along with my staff officer Premkumar, DySP and some constables. The DySP was instructed to get down at every stop and check the lock and the seal. At Chennai Central, the DIG, SSP and a battery of other ranks were waiting to welcome us.

The records reached safely, but I was rather distressed to learn that the constables who were sent by Head Office, Delhi had got down at Nagpur to quench their thirst (easy to guess about the nature of drink) and missed the train. They turned up two days later with long faces. Since the Zonal Office staff had ensured the safety of the records, the office started functioning straightaway. The negligent constables were packed off to Delhi after due admonition.

Consequent upon the Special Crime Branch of CBI vacating EVK Sampat Maligai and moving to Rajaji Bhavan, the Zonal Office shifted to EVK Sampat Maligai.

The year 1996 saw high profile cases pouring in one after another. Following a Public Interest Litigation, the High Court of Madras ordered a probe into the Cremation Sheds Scam. The construction of Cremation Sheds under the Jawahar Rozgar Yojna (JRY) was undertaken in all the districts of the state through nominated industrial cooperative societies. These societies were defunct and the work was actually entrusted to a contractor. As per the JRY, community assets were to be created by employing the local people and the involvement of any contractor/intermediary was banned. Work was also found to be substandard. Further, the type of work taken up did not figure in the guidelines listed in the manual. With the intention of benefitting one particular contractor the Government Order (GO) was issued by the Rural Development Department at the instance of the contractor. Some Collectors went ahead with giving work orders to the contractor even before the issue of the GO. Others simply implemented the GO. The promulgation of the GO itself was the common thread in the conspiracy.

The whole issue erupted when an Additional Collector in Madurai refused to obey his Collector to complete the balance payment as he found the work to be of substandard quality. Hence, initially the probe related to the tidings in Madurai district. Later, all the revenue districts were brought under the umbrella of investigation as per the directions of the High Court.

This was a mammoth task as over 2,000 sheds had to be evaluated with the help of civil engineers, apart from unravelling the conspiracy at macro as well as micro level (district). Enormous manpower and logistic support were required. Initially, such support was extended by TN Police. Finally, we were on our own.

We concentrated on the Madurai case and after obtaining sanction from the Central and State Governments chargesheet was laid in the court against the then minister for local administration, the secretary of the department, the director Rural Development, the collector Madurai, other officials and the contractor. This case has since been acquitted.

In another case, chargesheet was laid. However, with the return of the AIADMK Government in 2001 the CBI hit the wall, as sanction for prosecution was refused in the remaining cases. All the hard work by the investigating officers was demolished by just an administrative order.

Although one is expected to accept with dignity the decision of the authority competent to accord sanction for prosecution, there is no doubt that it dampens the spirit of the investigating officers. Miscarriage of justice is clearly discernible in cases where no sanguine reasons are adduced while declining sanction. There is no dearth of instances where this unfettered authority is wrongly exercised by the Government or bureaucrats to shield corrupt/errant officials. This provision requires a review and Section 197 CrPC as well as Section 19 of the Prevention of Corruption Act require a fresh look. If the competent authority refuses to accord sanction for prosecution for no right reason, the competent court should be empowered to take cognizance, if satisfied after going through the material placed before it.

Important cases registered during this period involved some senior bureaucrats. A Deputy Chairman of the Chennai Port Trust was alleged to have abused his authority to extend pecuniary benefit to a shipping company in the allotment of berth at the dock. Searches revealed concealed assets which led to a separate case for possession of assets disproportionate to his known sources of income. Both the cases were chargesheeted. The trial court acquitted both the cases. They have been taken up on appeal.

An income tax raid was conducted at the residence of a senior IAS officer, who was posted as the Chairman and Managing Director of Tamil Nadu Minerals, a State Government Undertaking. Since the disclosures were substantial CBI developed this information to project a case of disproportionate assets. After obtaining concurrence of the Tamil Nadu Government a case was registered accordingly. The officer put forth a strong explanation that the huge cash seized belonged to the Tamil Nadu Basketball Association and was available with him in his capacity as the President. Demolition of this plea required months of meticulous investigation. Still more difficult was the task of grappling with the claim that many of the resources belonged to his mother, who was a retired medical officer. While filing chargesheet, disproportion was projected at Rs 7.35 crore. The trial court discharged the case on the ground that sanction was necessary since he was reinstated following a Central Administrative Tribunal order. The trial court order was challenged in the High Court on a revision filed by CBI and the discharge order was set aside. Trial was in progress at the time of going for print.

Another important case under the PC Act handled by CBI, Chennai involved the Chairman and Managing Director of Neyveli Lignite Corporation. It was a case of disproportionate assets and registered with the approval of the Ministry of Coal. Right from the beginning CBI faced several hurdles in this case. It appears that the officer was tipped off and before the raid could be conducted the movable assets were removed. Further, the Ministry took three long years to decide upon some administrative action. In the meanwhile, an interesting development took place during investigation. Documents were submitted to explain substantial income generated from a corpus created through gifts received at the time of birth of the children. Investigation proved the documents to be fake which led to the registration of a separate case for cheating and falsification of documents. The trial court handed down a sentence, but the Session's Court set aside the conviction. Appeal filed by CBI is still pending in the High Court.

Chapter – 17

The Defenceless Tribe

Even where there is no infirmity in the investigation it does not rule out the accused nurturing a grievance against the investigating officer. Many such people, especially those who can afford eminent lawyers who in turn can impress the court, find a very easy way to harass the investigating officer (IO) by filing private complaints. Protection under Section 197 CrPC notwithstanding, these complaints are potential source of torture for the probe officer. Often these are referred to the local police for investigation under Section 156 CrPC. Sometimes the court takes cognizance straightaway and many courts rule that prior sanction is not necessary as the act in question is not related to the discharge of official duties. What is most agonising is that legal assistance is officially not available to the IO to defend himself against such frivolous prosecutions. He has to engage his own counsel and ask for reimbursement of the cost. Although this is a phenomenon affecting all police forces in the country, I found Bangalore to be conspicuous by the density of such events. In one case, an IPS officer filed a case against CBI officers who conducted search although the same was absolutely legal and carried out in the presence of responsible witnesses.

I cannot let one case pass without a detailed narration because it gave us a lot of pain. In a bank fraud case, registered at CBI Mumbai photographs of some wanted people were published in dailies. On seeing the photograph of a person named X an ASI of Bangalore branch informed the SP that he had seen him playing cricket on Sundays. The person was brought to CBI office in the morning. Inquiries revealed several features of the wanted person to match with those of the person available at Bangalore, such as:

1. Name
2. Both were A/C holders in PNB
3. Education background (both were engineers)
4. Identification mark
5. Photograph was same as appeared in the press
6. **Further, both had bank cases pending:** the wanted person was involved in a case of fraud and the person brought for inquiry was facing proceedings with the Debt Recovery Tribunal
7. Language was Telugu in both cases

The IO at Mumbai could be located with lot of difficulty, it being a Sunday. The IO asked for a photograph of the person to be faxed. On seeing the photograph he confirmed the similarity with the wanted person and asked him to be detained till the IO arrived at Bangalore the next day. In the meantime, lawyers and some retired CBI officer had lined up at the CBI office, demanding release of the person. In spite of a requisition from the IO the SP decided to let Mr X go home with the undertaking that he will present himself before the IO on his arrival from Mumbai. However, after the IO's visit to Bangalore and interaction with Mr X, he was found to be not the same person as the one wanted in the Mumbai case.

In this case, the SP had acted in absolute good faith. The case was not his. He had no prior knowledge about Mr X and hence there was no question of any personal motive. He was simply guided by the interest of the organisation.

Further, there was no ill-treatment to the person brought for enquiry. He was allowed to go home in spite of a specific request from the IO to detain him.

However, technically there was a violation of the guidelines issued by the Supreme Court in DK Basu's case. Mr X filed a complaint of harassment and unlawful detention with the National Human Rights Commission. The latter accepted the factual report from CBI highlighting the bona fides of the CBI action. However, guided by some former CBI officials Mr X filed a case in the High Court of Karnataka alleging contempt of the directions of the apex court in DK Basu's case. The case was filed one day prior to the expiry of the limitation period (365 days).

The case came up before a Division Bench and the Additional Solicitor General defended the CBI. Unconditional apology was tendered on behalf of CBI. Although the court agreed that everything was done in good faith, it concluded that trauma was caused to the petitioner which deserved compensation. Accordingly, the SP and two IOs were directed to compensate the petitioner in their individual capacity, by paying Rs 5000 each.

Chapter – 18

Contours of a High Profile Case

May 1996 saw a change of guard at Fort St George. Some time thereafter, the Chief Secretary received a complaint from the Director General, Investigation, Income Tax, Chennai which contained the following allegations.

Ms J Jayalalithaa, Chief Minister of Tamil Nadu had received a Demand Draft for $ 300000 drawn on ANZ Grindlays Bank, St Heliers, Jersey, Channel Islands, and claimed immunity under the foreign exchange remittance scheme 1991. As per Section 3(2)(b) of the scheme no immunity was available in this case.

On the occasion of her birthdays in 1990, 1991 and 1992 she has claimed to have received gifts amounting to Rs 1.71 crore in jewels, silver articles and Rs 2.4 crore in cash. The department has not accepted her contention that these were gifts and taken them as income.

This reference was sent to DGP Crime by the Chief Secretary and a case registered under Section 13(i)e of PC Act 1988 (possession of disproportionate assets). Sometime in August 1996, this case was sought to be transferred to CBI for investigation.

As per the procedure followed in CBI, when a case is referred by the state government the request is examined in head office and the Director decides whether the case is fit for CBI investigation or communicates his views to the Government of India. In case of acceptance, the Director also decides as to which branch of CBI should take up the case.

As the reply to the Government was being delayed, the Government, Department of Personnel, asked for quick action. Consequently, the Director sought the comments of JD South.

I came to a conclusion that in the absence of inputs concerning assets and expenditure a case of disproportionate assets cannot be projected. Further, the stand taken by the IT department that these gifts were treated as income will effectively bring down the disproportion. In addition, the registration of a separate case under Section 13(i)e PC Act by the State Vigilance and Anti-corruption will lead to overlapping the investigation. Then, there was the handicap that CBI was not empowered to investigate cases under Foreign Exchange Regulation Act 1973, in the absence of a notification from the Ministry of Finance under Section 5 of the Act. It appeared that in its present shape the FIR suffered from infirmities and I argued that prima facie Section 13(i)d (abuse of authority) was attracted and should be included, which was the aim of the investigation.

My views were endorsed by the legal adviser of CBI and approved by the Director Joginder Singh. The stand taken by CBI was not acceptable to the mandarins in the North Block and they turned the heat on the Director. The latter passed on the onus to the Joint Director that he was refusing to register the case. This was not a proper response. He was a party to the CBI's views submitted to the Government. If he had any other view he could have over-ruled the Joint Director and the Legal Advisor and straight away accepted the case. The officials in North Block developed a firm belief that I was the stumbling block and the Director's somersault drove me to a showdown with the Minister in charge. On his next camp to Chennai, I was asked to meet him. As expected, the meeting was a rather unpleasant one. Repeatedly he kept on referring to my comments mailed to the Director, constantly spitting fire on the stand taken by me. I attempted to explain to him that there was no refusal on our part and all that we did was to highlight the infirmities and infact, given suggestions to impart strength to the case. No amount of reasoning would convince him. When the accusations reached the level of questioning personal bona fides, I decided to walk out, clearly driving home that I was not prepared to suffer humiliation.

When I was walking upto the car, one of the aides of the Minister came rushing and requested me not to get angry. I drove off in a huff. The same aide called at home that the Minister had been briefed properly and that it would be appreciated if I met him the next day. I thought over the matter and decided to comply. The meeting turned out to be a cordial one and the discussion centred on the further course of action.

It was decided to thrash out the issues between CBI and the state government across the table. The meeting was chaired by the Chief Secretary, TN, KA Nambiar; who was assisted by Law Secretary, AK Rajan and the Special Counsel, N Natarajan; for the state government. The CBI team was comprised of the Special Director, DR Karthikeyan; the Joint Director, the author; the retainer counsel, P Rajamanickam; the DIG, S Seshadri; the SP, C Balasubramaniyam and the Senior Public Prosecutor, R Soundarajan.

The Chief Secretary and the special counsel for the state appeared to have already come to a conclusion that there was a prima facie case for disproportionate assets and the investigation agencies had only to wrap it up. I sought to explain that to launch an investigation in a case of this type there should be prima facie a projection of disproportion which should be arrived at after juxtaposing the income, expenditure and assets. The instant FIR lacked these details.

It was also pointed out that the existence of two FIRs under the same Section (13(i)e PC Act)—one pursued by the State V&AC and the other to be handled by CBI -would lead to complications. Further, the FIR sought to be transferred to CBI had two distinct components—one requiring investigation abroad and the other confined to domestic transactions alone. The Chief Secretary was of a firm view that the V&AC would cover the domestic portion, leaving only the allegation of receipt of three lakh dollars to the CBI for probe. I raised a question of law as to how could the allegations in the single FIR be split up and divided between two different agencies. Our Retainer Counsel offered a very unconvincing solution that a revised notification under Section 6 of the Delhi Special Police Act be issued by the TN Government restricting the scope of CBI probe to the receipt of $ three lakh alone. I opposed the idea on the ground that the FIR has been sent to the court and a composite disposal has to be placed befor the court, covering both the allegations. Further, the notification referred to the entire FIR and there cannot be a notification for a partial FIR. I was overruled and the Special Director agreed to the idea of a revised notification. We left the meeting promising to register the case forthwith. The entire FIR was taken into account. The promised revised notification never came. Obviously, the bureaucrats in Fort St George and North Block would have realised that it was not feasible.

One more issue had to be sorted out—whether CBI should look into the Foreign Exchange angle or not. Another meeting was convened—this one chaired by NK Singh, Union Revenue Secretary. He made it clear that this angle is within the purview of the Enforcement Directorate and CBI should furnish them the relevant documents. Thus, with initial hic-cups taken care of regular case number 50/96 registered by Anti-corruption Branch, Chennai started its eventful journey on the 2nd of October, 1996.

The case required evidence to be collected abroad. Initially, we tried to get information through the diplomatic channel as well as the Interpol. Subsequently, the Letter Rogatory was sent to the Channel Islands. The matter got stuck up here as the legal authorities had to be convinced about the dual criminality. The process took nearly three years and finally the requisite information was received. The report of investigation was submitted just before I completed my tenure and returned to the cadre in 2002. A final decision on the case was taken and chargesheet filed in 2006. The High Court discharged the case in 2012 on grounds of delay and paucity of evidence. The CBI is learnt to have filed a special leave petition in the Supreme Court.

Chapter - 19

Herbal Petrol

In 1999, Tamil Nadu was agog with the discovery of 'herbal petrol' by a rural scientist - Ramar Pillai. The latter, a drop-out from school, claimed that he tumbled upon the wonder herb on the hills near Srivilliputtur where his class was taken for a picnic. At the end of the day, the class teacher asked Pillai to extinguish the makeshift oven and throw it out in the bushes. When he threw the firewood, some leaves were seen aflame. Instantly, he inferred that the leaves contained combustible material and to develop it, he started a small laboratory at home, and took up deep studies in Chemistry. He was able to identify the chemical present in the herb and develop a process for commercial production of the fuel from this herb.

Politicians were quick to hail the discovery and honour the rural scientist. Some Chief Ministers publicly honoured him and announced cash rewards. The Swadeshi Jagaran Manch solidly backed him.

Ramar Pillai carried out experiments before public gatherings to produce herbal petrol, although in a small scale. The genuineness of the product was demonstrated by driving a two-wheeler with the help of the fuel produced. However, when the same experiment was performed before scientists, Ramar Pillai drew a blank as the committee stipulated that he had to use the equipment provided by it and not his own implements. The scientists smelt a rat that some trick was being played with the help of his equipments.

In spite of the scientific community holding back recognition, Ramar Pilllai, encouraged by politicians, political outfits and greedy businessmen went ahead with ambitious plans for commercial exploitation. He opened about 40 odd retail outlets in Chennai city. The first one was inaugurated amidst fanfare with prominent VIPs adoring the dais. They included the wife of the Chief Minister and Additional DGP, Law and Order.

Funded by unscrupulous petrol pump owners and politicians hoping to make quick money Ramar Pillai started making good business, auto-rickshaw drivers forming most of the customer base, who purchased the fuel at rates cheaper than that available at standard petrol bunks and charged their respective auto owners the normal rate. Perhaps only a few of them had a lurking doubt about the nature of the fuel sold and its potential in damaging the engines. They did not bother as the vehicles belonged to someone else. It is possible that some of the dealers also were aware that the material they were supplied for sale was anything but petrol.

One of those, who had invested in Ramar's business, was quick to realise the lack of foundation in his claim. When he confronted Ramar his doubts were confirmed that some organic chemicals were being sold in the name of herbal petrol. He decided to pull out of Ramar's network and passed on the information to CBI. To verify the information, I instructed the DIG CBI, Chennai to get some samples by deputing a decoy customer. The sample, purchased from a retail outlet, was sent to the Chennai Petroleum Corporation for analysis. Later another sample was sent to the Tamil Nadu Forensic Laboratory for similar analysis. Both the labs confirmed that the material being sold was a mixture of benzene and toluene and the components of petrol were missing. So, it became clear that Ramar Pillai was fooling the people and projecting the image of a rural scientist whose discovery could solve the energy crisis looming large due to the rapid depletion of the oil reserves.

There was another angle to this scam. As per the High Speed Diesel and Motor Spirit Rules 1998, the public sector oil companies have the responsibility of exercising vigil over the sale of adulterated petrol /diesel. Thus, there was gross negligence on the part of the designated officials in enforcing the above rule. It seemed probable that there was a nexus between these officials and Ramar Pillai. Accordingly, a case was registered against Ramar Pillai and unknown officials of public sector oil companies.

Raids were conducted at the godown hired by Ramar Pillai for production of herbal petrol and also at retail outlets. At the godown, several barrels of toluene and benzene were seized. Neither any petrol nor any herbs were seen at the so-called production center. Chemical analysis confirmed the contents of the barrels. Ramar Pillai was arrested and brought to CBI office, Shastri Bhavan for interrogation. He baffled the investigating officers with his self-acquired knowledge of chemistry. He claimed that the herbs contained an organic chemical called 'Lauric Acid' which provided the combustible material. On hearing this claim, I decided to join the interrogation hoping to draw upon my experience as a student and later as a teacher of organic chemistry in the university. For this, I had to refresh my knowledge on the subject and quickly got hold of 'Organic Chemistry' by IL Finar, the Bible for all students of the subject at graduation and post graduate levels.

I was adequately prepared to withstand the barrage of arguments on the feasibility of extracting petrol from herbs and its commercial production. Pillai broke down and admitted that he was using toluene and benzene only.

The expose hit the headline, but instead of bouquets, brickbats started pouring. I soon found myself on the firing line. Very senior members of the Union Cabinet started questioning the authority of the CBI in registering the case. The Director in turn, transmitted his tension to me and demanded an explanatory note. Within an hour I sent him a suitable reply, which prevented further queries. The annoyance of the then ruling party (BJP) was understandable since a semi-political outfit in Chennai providing umbrella to the rural scientist had allegience to the same party. A leader of this outfit called me up and virtually threatened me of dire consequences. Even a section of the media attempted to dub my action as a reflection of North Indian bias trying to put down a South Indian success story. However, the Chief Minister made a balanced comment "It appears that the scientists have not accepted Ramar Pillai's claim".

Undaunted by all threats the investigation progressed in the right earnest. The Madras Institute of Technology, Chrompet observed that the ignition temperature of the fuel was very high and that the fumes were carcinogenic. The high ignition temperature would definitely damage the engine of the vehicle and burn it out in a short span. Investigation covered a large network of investors which included politicians and businessmen running a chain of petrol bunks. However, no connivance on the part of the public sector oil companies could be established, although gross negligence was clearly visible with regard to their responsibility in checking the sale of adulterated petrol/diesel.

Chargesheet was filed against Ramar Pillai and four others including his foster mother Venudevi. The trial of the case has progressed very slowly and final disposal is still awaited. In the meantime, dramatic scenes have been witnessed outside the court. Ramar came to the brink of admitting the offence but his foster mother restrained him. Investors started pulling out, dealing a serious blow to the prosperous business.

Chapter - 20

Last Stint in Delhi

After an eventful tenure of seven years as Joint Director (South) CBI I returned to the state by the end of April 2002. Shortly before that I had met with a serious accident near Bangalore while proceeding to attend a meeting. My car had a collision with a bus, leading to hip fracture of my wife and I sustained serious head injury. We were initially treated as in-patient at St John's Medical College and later shifted to Madras Institute of Orthopaedics and Traumatology, Chennai. We returned home after 23 days and I could resume duty after another three weeks, but life was not the same again. My wife had to cope with a truncated femor head and I lost the faculty of smell.

When I reported for duty, the Chief Secretary, P Shankar, informed that they thought of giving me a light assignment, keeping the accident in view. That is how I landed up in the Uniformed Services Recruitment Board. A streamlined procedure was already in place. All that was required on the part of the Board was to keep a hawk's eye on the implementation. Care was required in the selection of officers of good reputation to head the sub-committees in charge of the first stage of recruitment, that is, certificate verification, physical measurement and physical efficiency test. Next important requirement was the need for secrecy in drafting and printing of question papers and their safe custody. I kept the master copy in my personal custody and installed a Duplo printer in my chamber so that the copies could be taken out in my presence, bunched up for various centres and sealed. The sealed packets were stored in steel boxes (earmarked for different centres), the boxes sealed and the keys kept in my custody. After office hours the room was locked and the key entrusted to the sentry, under acknowledgement. Armed escorts were summoned from various centres a couple of days prior to the written examination and the earmarked boxes handed over in sealed condition.

There was not much headache as far as evaluation of answer sheets was concerned since the entire process was computerised. The key was taken personally to the data centre only on the day of evaluation. Prior to that, transcription of data from the coded answer sheets to the master sheet was done by a dedicated team in the Board's office, under intense supervision and repeated cross-checking by senior officers.

During the tenure of just two years I attended three major recruitments - 5000 women PCs, 10,000 men constables and 736 women SIs. The hassle-free recruitments eased our tension as the previous recruitment of Sub Inspectors was mired in controversy.

In the meantime, orders came from the Government of India, appointing me as Additional Director in CBI, New Delhi. I felt elated and planned to leave immediately. That was not to be. Days rolled by, months passed - the relieving order was nowhere in sight. At the end of 3 months I had lost all hope and got reconciled to the thought of continuing with the cadre. The Ministry of Home Affairs was contemplating cancellation of the order. To my great surprise, immediately after the Lok Sabha election, the state government agreed to relieve me. Some bureaucrats advised me to leave immediately, without any publicity. I was also eager to go. So, I boarded IC-539 the next evening when the leaders in Delhi were intensely deliberating to find out a prime minister in the wake of the Congress President refusing to take up office.

I walked into Block 3, CGO Complex at Lodi Road on 19th of May, 2004 to start my third innings in CBI - an organisation whose ethos and culture had always been dear to my heart.

As per the prevalent organisational structure the investigative division of the CBI consisted of Anti-corruption, Special Crime and Economic Offences Wings, each supervised by an Additional Director. Perhaps in view of my previous experience, Director US Mishra entrusted me the Anti-corruption wing. The headquarter zone of this wing handled important and sensitive cases involving politicians, senior bureaucrats and high value contracts—such as defence deals. The other zones under my control also dealt with sensitive cases. Some of them were monitored by the Apex Court and the High Courts. Naturally these required very close attention by the senior mangement in CBI. All progress reports and affidavits had to be drafted with extreme caution, vetted by the Director of Prosecution and cleared by the Director CBI himself. Some of these cases warranted consultation with the Attorney General and the Solicitor General as well as personal attendance by officers upto the rank of Additional Director. We had to grapple with a lot of tension.

One such case was the Taj Corridor probe entrusted by the Supreme Court. The project known as the Taj Heritage Corridor Project was initiated by the Government of Uttar Pradesh. The main purpose for which the same was undertaken was to divert River Jamuna and reclaim 75 acres of land between Agra Fort and the Taj Mahal and use the reclaimed land for constructing food plazas, shops and amusement parks. The said activities on the part of the Uttar Pradesh Government were brought to the notice of the Apex Court. An exception thereto was taken and an inquiry by CBI ordered. On consideration of the CBI report the Supreme Court directed registration of FIR and further investigation as per law. The role of the then Chief Minister of UP Kumari Mayawati and senior bureaucrats like the Secretary Environment, Secretary to CM, Chief Secretary and Minister of Environment UP had to be probed. The scope of the inquest covered the favours extended to a contractor M/s Ishvakoo through the National Projects Construction Corporation and releasing a sum of Rs 17 crore as the first instalment for the construction of Taj Corridor at Agra. The amount was released without preparing a detailed project report and approval of the Cabinet Committee on economic affairs, Government of India.

The case was investigated by the Lucknow branch of CBI. After meticulous investigation the IO filed his report without any specific recommendation on the disposal of the case leaving the decision to the hierarchy. With inputs from the Senior Public Prosecutor, the Superintendent of Police, the Deputy Legal Advisor and the DIG Lucknow the reports were examined in the head office. The Additional Legal Advisor, the Joint Director, the Director of Prosecution and the Additional Director (myself) participated in this mammoth exercise. The senior public prosecutor and the Director of Prosecution held that there was no case for prosecution whereas the other law officers, namely, the DLA and the ALA along with executive officers were unanimous that undue favours had been shown to the contractor by the public servants who abused their authority. Of course, there were minor differences on the individuals to be prosecuted. Because of conflicting views and considering the personalities involved, it was a difficult task for the Director to come to a final conclusion. No amount of discussion would help. Finally, the case was referred to the Learned Attorney General of India. The latter agreed with the opinion of the senior PP and the Director of Prosecution. The Director CBI ordered closure of the case while recommending disciplinary action against some bureaucrats for procedural lapses.

Even before the closure report could be filed in the competent court at Lucknow the information relating to the proposed action, as indicated in the status report got publicised, and proved to be red rag to the litigants who lost no time in agitating the matter before the Bench and contesting the decision of the CBI. When the matter came up before the three-judge Bench privilege was claimed in respect of the opinion of the AG and the Solicitor General appeared on behalf of CBI. Along with the investigating officer, the DIG, Joint Director and the Director of Prosecution I attended court on several dates. It was a good experience listening to eminent counsels like KK Venugopal and the Solicitor General.

In view of the plethora of opinions in this case the Apex Court desired the Central Vigilance Commissioner to tender his opinion. Arguments were advanced claiming that the decision of the investigating agency could be contested only after closure report was filed in the competent court. It was also pointed out that the CVC had no authority to question the nature of disposal given to a case by the CBI.

In compliance with the court order the CVC went through the case records and tendered his opinion. The same appeared to be in line with the stand taken by the Additional Director (the author). The Bench consisting of three judges rejected the arguments of the Solicitor General and the counsel for the former Chief Minister that the court had no authority to direct the investigating agency on the nature of disposal and ordered action as per the recommendations of the SP CBI. The Bench held that on completion of investigation, the formation of the opinion whether or not there is a case to place the accused on trial should be that of the officer in charge of the police station and none else. It also held that according to the CBI manual the Superintendent of Police is in charge of the police station. Hence, it directed the CBI to place the evidence/material collected by the investigating team alongwith the report of the SP as required under Section 173 CrPC before the concerned court who will decide the matter in accordance with law. None of the other opinions, including that of the Learned Attorney General or the CVC was to be forwarded to the court.

Everyone expected a quietus to the issues raised in the public interest litigation. Even when the matter was pending in the Supreme Court some developments took place in the CBI head office with US Mishra superannuating Vijay Shankar took his place. Shortly thereafter, the CVC Board convened to consider the promotion of the two Additional Directors (myself and JK Dutt) to the rank of Special Director, both being in the central panel for appointment as Director General of Police in the Government of India.

While Vijay Shankar informed me about my selection, a week later I came to know that contrary to the message conveyed by the Director, the CVC Board had recommended curtailment of my tenure in CBI. In fact, MHA had already proposed my appointment as Director General (investigation) in the National Human Rights Commission. As I preferred to get back to the cadre, I immediately met Vijay Shankar with a petition for repatriation. Regarding the wrong information given earlier about my selection as Special Director a funny clarification was given that due to cross talks going on in the board meeting the discussion with regard to my curtailment of tenure had escaped his notice. At the same time, he refused to accept my petition till a firm communication was received.

When I met P Shankar, Central Vigilance Commissioner, he confirmed the fact and explained that he was given to understand that I was not willing to continue in CBI—a damned lie. When I asserted that I had not expressed my unwillingness before anyone, Mr Shankar was taken by surprise. He made a feeble attempt to retrieve the situation by calling up Brahma Dutt the Additional Secretary, Department of Personnel, but gave up on being informed that the file had already moved to the Cabinet Committee on Appointments. It was rather strange that the CVC never bothered to cross-check with me whether I was willing or not to continue in CBI.

By the time my petition was forwarded to the Government, orders for NHRC were already on the way. I had no option but to join NHRC. The MHA sat over my petition for over three months, not bothering to even give a rejection or endorsement. If there was a global competition in the art of confabulations, no one can deny the first place to some of our bureaucrats.

In the subsequent days, there were further developments in the Taj Corridor case, as learnt from the press. The CBI sought sanction for prosecution from the Government of Uttar Pradesh in respect of Mayawati and Shamsuddin Siddique, Minister for Environment and other bureaucrats along with the contractor.

The authority competent to accord sanction in respect of the Chief Minister is the Governor. Here the CBI hit the wall. His Excellency declined to accord sanction. The *amicus curiae* raised the following issues. (1) Legal validity in CBI seeking the sanction. 2. A copy of the sanction order of the Governor to be furnished for scrutiny. 3. Legal validity of the order denying the sanction. 4. Sanction order is in public domain. Hence, cannot be classified as secret.

The Apex Court observed that in this case they were concerned with ensuring proper and honest performance of duty by CBI and their observations and reasons were confined only to that aspect of the case. If no sanction of the Governor was required, or if he has committed an error in passing the said order, the appropriate court would be entitled to deal therewith, but not the Apex Court.

The High Court has however taken cognizance of a petition filed against the action of the Governor.

Another case which required senior officers to brief the Solicitor General and attend Supreme Court was a case of disproportionate assets pending against Lalu Prasad

Yadav and his wife Rabri Devi, both former Chief Ministers of Bihar, in the Special Court of Patna. In the trial court, Ansari, senior public prosecutor, was appearing on behalf of CBI. Prosecution arguments had been completed and the case was pending for defence arguments.

In the meanwhile, one Oma Shankar Sharma was appointed as Special Counsel for CBI cases pending in Bihar and Jharkhand courts. He was assigned this particular case along with other cases. Changing the prosecutor midstream gave rise to a serious controversy and one Rajiv Singh Lallan filed public interest litigation in the Apex Court. Eminent counsel Mukul Rohtagi appeared on his behalf, the Solicitor General represented CBI and Ram Jethmalani appeared on behalf of Lalu Prasad. It was a great experience hearing the eminent counsels whose eloquence matched each other. Although changing the prosecutor was an administrative step and purely within the competence of Director CBI, the litigants kept on asserting this to be a motivated act with a view to help the accused. Apart from projecting our bona fides before the Bench the previous prosecutor was reattached with the case. Hence, the PIL was disposed of.

Yet another issue brought before the Apex Court was the matter pertaining to the posting of the particular person as Special Judge CBI to try the case. His credentials were questioned highlighting his allegiance to the accused. The service records of the special judge were perused by the Bench and views of the Chief Justice Patna High Court, who had made the appointment, obtained. The Apex Court observed that Yogendra Prasad, Special Judge, who was trying the case, had been elevated to the rank of District Judge, thus necessitating the appointment of a substitute. This process was completed without contravention of any rules. The standing committee of the High Court had approved the selection. Further; there was nothing against the honesty and integrity of the person selected. Hence, there was no illegality/ irregularity in the selection.

Serious allegations were raised about the disposal of an income tax matter in favour of Lalu Prasad Yadav and

Rabri Devi. It appears that Rabri Devi had claimed income from dairy farming, rentals etc which was questioned by the assessing authority. She went on to appeal to the Income Tax Appellate Tribunal (ITAT). The incumbent member was replaced by a pliable officer, who was on the verge of retirement, who decided the appeal in favour of the accused. The department did not file an appeal. The Apex Court observed that the incumbent member had requested a transfer and was already facing disciplinary action. The court found no irregularity in the appointment of the successor. Further, the income tax department had consulted the Ministries of Finance and Law before deciding not to file an appeal against the order of ITAT.

CBI had obtained sanction for prosecution from the Governor of Bihar in respect of Lalu Prasad Yadav, the then Chief Minister. No permission was obtained from the Speaker to prosecute Rabri Devi. The validity of the sanction in respect of Lalu Prasad Yadav and absence of sanction in respect of Rabri Devi were agitated by the accused before the High Court of Patna. The full bench upheld the stand of the prosecution. The Supreme Court dismissed the appeal filed by the accused against the order of the High Court. After all the legal battle, the Special Judge went ahead with the remaining part of the trial and exonerated Lalu Prasad Yadav and Rabri Devi. CBI did not consider it a case fit for filing appeal. The Government of Bihar considered it to be miscarriage of justice and filed an appeal against the acquittal. The Apex Court observed that in a case investigated by CBI the state government had no *locus standi*. Thus, the curtains came down on an epic proceeding which lasted for twelve years.

During the pendency of this issue I had to leave CBI on transfer.

Cracking a case of unfair practice adopted by some candidates in a competitive examination was a novel experience. It was the entrance examination for admission to the Delhi College of Engineering. By in-depth scrutinies of the marksheets of the successful candidates the authorities were able to notice identical marks obtained by a group of candidates. Further scrutiny revealed identical answering pattern. Suspecting foul play the matter was referred to CBI. The High Court also came in the picture and started monitoring the probe since some successful candidates whose results were withheld, had approached the court.

The credit for unravelling the mystery of this marks scandal goes to the Anti-Corruption Branch, Delhi under the supervision of RK Dutta, Joint Director.

The mastermind of this racket was an ex–student of the same college, now employed as Assistant Manager in Maruti Udyog. In league with his elder brother, an engineer and eleven other engineering and MBA students the accused was able to establish contact with fifty-two candidates for the Common Entrance Examination (CEE) 2005. They used the loopholes and exploited the lenient procedure of examination. The candidates were asked by the accused to take their mobiles inside the examination hall, so that they could receive the SMS containing the answer key from the accused.

Even though there was an announcement not to keep mobiles there was no physical checking and all the fifty-two candidates were able to carry the mobiles as instructed by the king pin Pankaj Dahiya during a briefing session two to three days prior to the examination. New SIM cards were provided to them during such briefing and the examinees instructed to activate them before the examination and destroy the same immediately after the exam. They were also asked to dispose off the handsets after use in the hall.

Dummy candidates were arranged to smuggle out the question papers immediately after commencement of the exam. Superintendents of two centres lodged police complaints in this regard. At Vidya Jain School, Rohini one of the accused scaled over the boundary wall and escaped on a bike after snatching the question paper from one genuine candidate.

Pankaj Dahiya along with other accused arranged a team of talented students of IIT Roorkee and Delhi College of Engineering at three centres to solve the questions within an hour and sent the answers to the aspiring students through SMS for which they were charged Rs 4 lakh each. The case is in the court now.

Just as a correct diagnosis renders extreme satisfaction to a physician, this case gave us a sense of real achievement. Based on CBI's findings the authorities were able to chalk out preventive measures for future. The High Court accepted the CBI report to its satisfaction.

Just the previous year, the same unit of CBI had smashed a similar racket concerning the Combined Entrance Test (CAT) for admission to various management institutes including IIMs. In this case, of course, the question paper was already smuggled out of the printing press and the success of CBI revolved around an excellent information network. On a tip off, a surprise check was conducted by CBI officials at Hotel Shanti Palace, Mahipalpur, New Delhi on 22.11.03. Different sections of question papers reported to be of the CAT examination to be held on 23.11.03 were recovered from the possession of five candidates taking up this exam. These candidates were brought to the hotel by a gang of four persons headed by Kumar Suman Singh alias Ranjit Singh of Patna for handing over the question papers.

The question paper was printed at the Institute of Banking and Personnel Selection, Mumbai. After printing, the question papers were handed over to a contractor for binding operations. One Sanjeev Kumar was employed as a daily wage worker with the contractor. He was able to smuggle out one paper from the bundle and hand it over to the gang which organised the crime by contacting and helping the candidates. Sanjeev Kumar collected Rs 21.25 lakh from the organisers who, in turn, charged the examinees Rs 2 to 4 lakh each. The case is since chargesheeted.

Chapter - 21

Posting in NHRC

Subsequent to the CVC board curtailing my tenure in CBI on the basis of an imaginary presumption that I was not willing to continue, the MHA pursued my posting in the National Human Rights Commission, ignoring my plea for repatriation. The loyal soldier, I have always been, I said good bye to CBI and on 16th of March, 2006 walked up the stairs of Faridkot House, New Delhi to head the investigation wing of the Commission.

In spite of the initial hesitation to take up this assignment, I decided to put in my heart and soul behind the job once I took the charge. The Chairman, Justice Anand and the other members namely, Justice Shivraj Patil, Justice Rao, RS Kalha and PC Sharma warmly welcomed me and treated me with respect. Most of the work related to instances of custodial death or torture referred to by the members. The pendency was mind boggling. Liquidation of the backlog within a short period was a Herculean task; however substantial reduction was certainly not an ambitious attempt.

Members of the Commission would call for reports from the investigation wing. In turn, reports would be called from the State Police authorities. These had to be analysed and a report submitted to the Law Division. The Law Division would put up draft proceedings to the concerned member. Important cases were referred by the members to the full commission. During my tenure, a decision was taken to get the proceedings drafted by the investigation division. This gave me an opportunity to standardise the format which in turn helped in speeding up the disposal.

The initial message from the concerned state, inquest report, postmortem examination, the magisterial inquiry report and the report on the action taken against delinquent officials usually formed the basis of the proceedings. Abnormal delay was noticed on the part of state officials in furnishing the requisite information. Reports written in languages other than English and Hindi had to be translated into English. This also involved considerable delay. Lot of time was consumed in obtaining clarifications on sketchy reports received, especially from the northern belt. Lack of seriousness was apparent. Magisterial inquiry reports were sometimes less than a page along with no details on the examination of witnesses or documents. The magistrate nominated was often in the rank of Deputy Tashildar only. In comparison, the Southern States were found to attach great importance to cases of this nature. The magisterial inquiry was conducted by a Sub-Divisional Magistrate and the report invariably was exhaustive. These states scrupulously followed the statutory provisions laid down in the Police Standing Orders and the Jail Manual. Once any instance of custodial death or torture or rape is reported the District Magistrate orders a magisterial inquiry. The report is submitted to the Government through the District Magistrate alongwith his/her recommendations for acceptance or otherwise. Although the process is time consuming and the application of mind by senior level functionaries is ensured. As per a revised procedure inquiry is held by a Judicial Magistrate.

Full commission used to be convened twice/thrice a week. The Director General (Investigation) and his deputy were required to attend these proceedings. It was observed that some of the cases were of seven to ten years vintage—a rather perplexing phenomenon. Most of these cases were pending for want of supplementary reports on the implementation of the interim compensation awarded or the outcome of disciplinary action against delinquent officials. Apart from the lackadaisical attitude of the state officials, the inadequacy of the staff at the commission was also responsible for the slow disposal of some cases. With the setting up of Human Rights Commission in more and more states, the situation is bound to improve. The NHRC generally does not pursue cases already taken cognizance of by the concerned State Human Rights Commission.

With a pretty long exposure in the field incidents involving custodial violence were not unknown to me. However, the magnitude of this malady turned out to be a shocking revelation as I got the first opportunity to view the nationwide picture by virtue of my assignment in NHRC. Reports received from the states made painful reading. Reports on complaints of illegal detention presented a distinct pattern. In many cases, it would be explained that the complainant or victim was brought to the police station merely for questioning in a case and let off. Corresponding entries in the general diary would be cited as evidence, little realising the lack of conviction in such assertion as manipulation in the general diary as a usual practice is common knowledge. In cases of this type atleast the illegal custody is curtailed. Worse is the scenario where the general diary is kept pending to accommodate suitable entries and cases are booked as soon as the victim's relatives dash off complaints. Plain reading of the FIR would reveal the artificial nature of the text. Even where the reporting authorities concede some lapses on the part of their subordinate officials it is frustrating to note that the delinquent is let off with a warning or censure even where illegal detention is proved. The Supreme Court had laid down elaborate guidelines to be observed while taking anyone in custody. These guidelines seem to be flouted nonchalantly by the law enforcement agencies. If only the supervisory officers keep a watch on the strict adherence to the eleven commandments (DK Basu case), the age-old malaise is definitely going to come down. Severe action on delinquents is also the need of the day, if some deterrence is to be generated. We were able to prevent a child marriage in the nick of the moment by utilising the good offices of the District Magistrate.

The short but eventful stint in NHRC gave me an opportunity to rededicate myself to the ideal of human rights and give a direction to the Tamil Nadu Police as its Chief to attach utmost priority to the preservation of human rights.

Chapter - 22

The Final Innings

When I left the state on the 18th of May 2004, it was lock, stock and barrel. I had taken it for granted that I would be signing off from the premier investigation agency of Government of India which I had dreamt of leading some day. I had no inkling that I would be required to play my last innings at Chennai. As for the dream, it turned out to be a day one, thanks to a very narrow interpretation of the Supreme Court order regarding the selection of Director CBI (in C Dinakar's case) by the CVC Board. The Supreme Court order stipulated that for the selection, "Ordinarily, four senior most batches of IPS officers of seniority, integrity and exposure to anti-corruption work should be considered". When the CVC Board met to select a successor (a panel) for US Mishra, who was superannuating, officers of batches 1967 to 1970 formed the seniormost four. The Board ignored the saving expression, 'Ordinarily', which meant that there was no bar for considering more batches in exceptional circumstances. It was unfair not to consider 1971 batch of officers, who were empanelled by Government of India for appointment as DGP in the central police organisations. The outgoing Director gave me the impression that he was going to take up this stand and recommend our batch to be considered. Apparently, he had changed his mind later. Because of the rigid interpretation of the Apex Court order our batch got ignored and there ended my dream and I had to leave CBI for NHRC.

My interaction with the Home Secretary, VK Duggal, and the Special Secretary, GS Rajagopal, who happened to be my batch mate, gave me clear indications that they had no intention of allowing me to get back to the cadre. It was clear that I would have to see through the remaining period of my service at NHRC. Just when I got into the groove and started streamlining the work of the investigation division of NHRC, the elections in Tamil Nadu were over. There was a change of guard at Fort St George and the new Government headed by Chief Minister M Karunanidhi was looking for an officer to head the TN Police in place of AX Alexander who was to retire shortly.

Even before the counting of votes began the trend was well known and it was clear that DMK would be forming the Government for the fifth time. A senior police officer from Chennai called me on 8th of May 2006 and asked me to contact a senior bureaucrat, who was tipped to occupy an important post. The latter indicated that there was a plan to call me back and wanted to know if I was willing. Since I had already submitted my petition for repatriation, I readily agreed.

The new Government was sworn in on the 13th of May and the same day orders were issued appointing me as the DGP. The Government of India was requested to relieve me forthwith. Pending my repatriation my batch mate KP Jain was made in charge. The Government of India took some time to process the request from TN Government and issue relieving orders. All these days there were frantic queries from Chennai about my possible arrival. Finally, I could leave Delhi on the 24th evening and take charge as the 20th DGP of the State with effect from 25th May, 2006.

Return to the State was a refreshing change after a shocking exposure to the bureaucratic politics at the national level. I picked up human rights as the main theme of police administraion. With this in view, I revived the Police Image Project which I had once coordinated as IGP, Planning and Coordination. I nominated the IGP Technical Services to be the Project Coordinator. CV Rao, the then incumbent, did a splendid job to locate the previous circulars and update the instructions in the backdrop of guidelines issued by the Apex Court in DK Basu case. An exhaustive list of 'dos and donts' that constitute good police image, was prepared. Two Inspectors with good track record were selected in each district to function as Project Inspectors. They were assembled at the headquarters and briefed thoroughly on their role in the project. I took up this opportunity to address them on the importance of human rights. These officers, in turn, took up in right earnest the task of catechising the subordinate ranks at the station level. Monthly reports were called and their performance monitored.

The scheme generated a good degree of interest among zonal IGs, range DIGs and District SPs. They were encouraged to try innovative ideas to improve the police image and any success achieved was discussed in the monthly coordination meetings and other officers were directed to emulate.

The IG Central zone assembled a group of head constables from all the police stations in his zone. After suitable briefing they were despatched to various stations as decoy complainants. Care was taken to send them to stations where they had not worked earlier and their identity was unknown. After three days, they were reassembled and asked to narrate their experience. Most of them had a tale of woe and eleven of them reported even physical abuse. The acidic experience prompted the lot to take a pledge that they will not indulge in such behaviour in future.

Discontent in personal life has a profound effect on a policeman's performance at the public interface. Hence, the importance of welfare, one area we thought we could take some initiative, was to help the children of policemen seek placements commensurate with their educational background. The IGs Central and Norther Zones and Commissioner Trichy displayed tremendous initiative and the job fairs organised by them proved to be a great success. I attended one such event at Trichy and personally handed over appointment letters to scores of wards of policemen. The initiative went well with the constabulary and I am sure, it helped raise their level of contentment and performance.

Within the short span of about fifteen months I remained the police chief, the state witnessed a series of VVIP visits and landmark events. Visits by the President and Prime Minister are a common feature and there is nothing new to write about their security arrangements as the same are elaborately mentioned in the Blue Book. The issue which was of serious concern was the mind-boggling traffic of Chennai City and the tall task of ensuring smooth passage of the VVIP carcade without serious detriment to the normal traffic. The problem got compounded when the VVIP got engaged in multiple programmes organised at different locations which required criss crossing the city during peak hours. Sometimes, other VIPs like the Governor, the Chief Minister and Union Ministers joined one or more functions and separate route *bandobast* had to be organised for them. Blocking the normal traffic at intersections and releasing it immediately on passage of the convoy, required clockwise precision and fool-proof skill. The city traffic wing headed by Sunil Kumar, Joint Commissioner rose upto every occasion commendably.

Instances which readily come to mind include a visit by Dr APJ Abdul Kalam, the President of India, which comprised of five functions at different locations spread over the entire city. On another occasion, we had to organise the route *bandobast* at a notice of barely two and half hours for the road journey from Nellore to Chennai. A gigantic task cropped up before TN Police when a string of visits to industrial houses was planned for Dr Manmohan Singh, Prime Minister and Sonia Gandhi in Sriperumbudur area. The Prime Minister and the Congress President were to use the helicopter from Chennai airport to Oragadam, the first function place. The Governor and the CM preferred to converge there using the road route. The next functions were to be covered by road by the entire enoturage visiting Rajiv Gandhi Memorial, Rajiv Gandhi Youth Foundation, M/s Nokia and M/s Flextronics. This required up and down travel on the National Highway by the entire party. Separate arrangements had to be made for the Chief Minister's visit to St Gobain. The PM hopped back to the airport using the chopper whereas the Governor returned to Raj Bhavan by road and the CM proceeded to Mahaballipuram before returning to the city, all by road. One can easily imagine the efforts taken by TN Police in ensuring smooth passage for different VVIPs and causing least inconvenience to the travellers on the National Highway and State Highway. This was a feather in the cap of Sunil Kumar, Joint Commissioner Traffic and K Radhakrishnan, IG North Zone.

One incident, which gave us anxious moments, took place close on the heels of the day long visit of his Excellency the President of India. The last leg of the visit -interview with selected individuals and groups -was slated at the airport terminal before take off to Delhi. Everything was going as per schedule till about 10 pm when an anonymous call was received at Chennai City Police South Control that there was a bomb on board. Although the entire pre-take off drill had been carried out meticulously, and most of the members of the entourage and the baggage already on board, there was no question of ignoring the disturbing message. The VVIP, who was in the process of completing the interviews, was informed of the developments by the Military Secretary. There was going to be considerable delay in departure as the team members and the entire baggage had to be offloaded and anti-sabotage check carried out afresh. Unperturbed by the chain of events, the VVIP kept himself pre-occupied, preparing for the next day's programme at Delhi.

By the time security clearance could be given and His Excellency could board, it was 2 am in the morning. It was amazing to see the ever tranquil First Citizen take leave of each one of us, the warmth of his handshake not reduced even a degree as we had felt on his arrival.

While the safe journey of the VVIP received the first priority, simultaneously different teams of Chennai City Police had already fanned out to locate the sender of the hoax call. From the number recorded at the control room it transpired that Tata Telecom happened to be the service provider at the caller's end. Quickly, the installation was traced to be that of a prominent jewellery shop in the city. On locating the shop, the investigating team tumbled upon further evidence in the form of a closed circuit television in running condition which was presumably used to screen the customers. Replay of the CCTV threw out profile of a youngster entering the telephone booth at the precise time in question. He was identified to be an employee of the shop. Investigation revealed that another young man, a friend of the culprit, was present at the time of making the call. His interrogation revealed that the accused wanted to play a prank on the police department and went ahead to accomplish his plan in spite of being advised against by his friend. The prankster was picked up and the case was cracked by Chennai City Police within 24 hours under the able stewardship of the COP Mrs Letika Saran.

The All India Police Duty Meet was held at Chennai in January 2007. Teams from various States and Central Police Organisations assembled here. The combined population of the contingents was to the tune of 1000. Dog squads were part of several teams. Reception of the team members, arranging accommodation and transport for such a huge number proved to be a mammoth task indeed. The organising committee did a remarkable job on all fronts. The efficiency of this committee and the subcommittees was of such order that there was not a single complaint from anyone of the teams. Arranging accommodation was a serious problem. Fortunately, brand new residential complexes were available at Mylapore and Nungambakkam for Chennai City Police. These were just awaiting inauguration and allotment. We decided to defer the inauguration till the completion of the Duty Meet and utilise the quarters for housing the teams. After personal inspection of these blocks by me and the COP they were earmarked for the teams. Basic amenities like water, power and messing arrangements were ensured. The TN Police, patronised by a magnanimous and understanding administration, did not fail to live up to its proverbial reputation of a good host, a fact acknowledged by all team captains at the Bada Khana held on the penultimate day. Apart from receiving accolades for organising the meet to perfection, TN Police will ever cherish sweet memories of bagging 18 medals including 8 gold and the overall championship.

A ghastly tragedy that shook everybody and will be difficult to forget was the accidental explosion that took place at Sendoor village in Villupuram district, situated near Tindivanam on the National Highway 45 (Chennai to Dindigul). Sixteen lives were lost and 22 people sustained severe injuries. The incident took place at about 11.30 hours on 7.4.07. On receipt of information, I rushed to the site along with RN Sawani, ADGP, HQ. K Radhakrishnan, IG North Zone had proceeded ahead and ADGP Law and Order KVS Murthy, cut short his leave and joined us at Tindivanam. My mobile kept on ringing the entire stretch of the journey, media people trying to ascertain the reason for the blast and whether extremists were involved. The callers included several local and national channels. It was rather surprising to receive enquiries from *Al Jazeera*. I kept on disseminating the first hand information which ruled out involvement of extremists.

The blast scene wore a gory look. Fragments of bodies could be seen even at a distance of fifty metres from the point of explosion. Roofs of houses adjoining the National Highway were blown off and the engine block of the jeep used by the transporter was jettisoned 50 metres away across the National Highway. The exact point of explosion was the junction of a road coming from Alapakkam and the National Highway. A crater 3 ft deep and diameter 6 feet was created. The forensic experts were busy collecting scientific clues. Electronic and print media with scores of cameramen thronged the entire place.

It was crystal clear from the spot of investigation that the consignment which had exploded, belonged to a licenced dealer Sekar, owner of Sri Shakti Explosives. He had a magazine located in a village 3 kilometres east of the blast scene. We visited the magazine also. Records revealed that a consignment of 200 kgs of slurry explosives, 375 metres of fuse and 150 electric detonators was loaded into the jeep-cum-van TN TCQ 3033 specially designed for transporting explosives. This consignment was sold to SPL Infrastructure Private Ltd, a contractor who required it for blasting boulders along the National Highways, necessitated for widening work. The mistake committed by the consignor was to load the explosive and the detonators in the same vehicle which was against the rules. The employees of the consignor – Babu (driver), Balaraman and Kumar travelled in the vehicle. It was around 11.30 hours when they reached the NH junction at Sendur. By that time, the portion of the slurry explosive started smouldering. On seeing the smoke the occupants panicked, jumped out of the vehicle and started crying for help. Immediately, lot of people gathered and attempted to douse the smoke by throwing sand on the heap of explosives. This mechanical shock triggered off the blast facilitated by the presence of the detonators. Sixteen people including the employees of the consignor died on the spot and two succumbed to injuries on the way to the hospital.

Based on the investigation factual information was given out to the media. The leader of the opposition, who also happened to visit the place, was quick to contest the findings and asserted that RDX was used and extremists were involved. To our great relief, the Chief Minister gave us solid support and an article in *Murasoli*, countering the insinuations levelled. A similar statement issued by the Minister of Power appeared in *Dina Thanthi* and other vernacular dailies. When I called on the CM to express my gratitude for his gracious gesture, he just smiled and asked me not to bother about such criticism.

Luckily for us, Nagappan, manager of Sri Sakti Explosives and his assistant Annamalai were traced the very next day and allowed to be interviewed by the electronic and print media including the channel functioning as the mouthpiece of the main opposition. The reporters grilled the employees of the consignor at great length but failed to extract any nod on their wild imagination as regards the involvement of extremists or the explosive turning out to be RDX. On the contrary, they confirmed the entire sequence worked out by the investigating team which turned out splendid work under the leadership of K Radhakrishnan, IG North Zone. Mr Periayah SP was able to crack the case within 24 hours. The fact that the case was one of an accident caused by negligence and no extremist was involved came as a great relief to one and all. The Forensic Lab confirmed the explosive to be slurry and not RDX.

The licencee, Sekar was detained under the National Security Act, but the Advisory Board quashed the detention as the explosion was only an accident. The legal issues were examined in detail. It was felt that under the existing law only sections of Indian Penal Code concerning rash and negligent act (Sections 286, 268 and 304 A) were attracted. The same provided lenient punishments. The incident emanated from an act of criminal negligence and stiffer punishment as under the Explosive Substances Act was called for to deal with such cases. This required a liberal text in Sections 3 and 4 where the expression 'unlawfully and maliciously' is required to be amended to read 'unlawfully or maliciously'. Such a law also exists in Bangladesh.

Further, in Canadian Law a legal duty is cast on one in possession or control of an explosive substance to use reasonable care to prevent bodily harm or death or damage to property by that explosive substance. If breach of that duty leads to death or is likely to cause death, the punishment is life imprisonment. If the damage is bodily harm, or to property punishment is upto 14 years imprisonment. Suggestions were sent to the Government to amend our law accordingly. Such changes were also recommended by the one man enquiry Commission.

The 'Q' branch headed by Davidson, SP and later Ashok Kumar turned out some splendid work ably-guided by AK Viswanathan DIG. They were covering the activities of left-wing extremists as well as Sri Lankan militants, especially the LTTE.

The Naxalite movement first made inroads in the State in the early seventies under the leadership of Kaliaperumal, a teacher from South Arcot district, Kothandaraman, a lawyer from Madras, L Appu, Coimbatore, Thiagarajan, Thanjavur, Tamilvanan and Kannamani, both from Dharmapuri, who were initiated by Charu Mazumdar, the Naxalite guru, during his visit to Hogenekkal. Incidentally, I had the opportunity to have a glimpse of the legendary Charu Mazumdar at Calcutta. For Bharat Darshan our group had been to eastern India and the Naxalite leader had landed in the police net just when we reached Calcutta. During our visit to the City Police Headquarters the Commissioner, RN Chatterjee, permitted us to have a look at the Naxalite leader on condition that we do not attempt any conversation. Two constables were stationed inside the lock-up to guard against any untoward incident. Charu Mazumdar was rather ill and appeared to be a skeleton wrapped in skin. He would not sleep for days together. The doctor was injecting pethidine when we saw him. His bulging eyes frightened us. The next day he passed away.

The Naxalite movement in Tirupattur, North Arcot district, owes its genesis to the efforts of Tamilvanan and Kannamani. Having set the movement in motion and personally wanted in half a dozen cases of murder and rioting, they shifted their focus to Tirupattur, adjoining Krishnagiri, the seat of their early operations. While AM Kothandaraman and Tamilvanan continued to evade the police for long, L Appu and Kannamani were killed in encounters and Kaliaperumal had to serve life sentence.

Sivalingam, a loco driver at Jolarpet railway station, was dismissed in 1975 for wagon looting and rioting. He was roped in by Tamilvanan and Kannamani to boost the movement in Tirupattur area. Seeralan was one of the first disciples of Sivalingam. They spearheaded the attack on Appaswamy Chettiar of Athipallam, Dharmapuri. This has been narrated in the chapter concerning my experience in Dharmapuri district.

Subsequent years saw a spurt in Naxalite activity. An operating zone was created in the trough between Javadi and Yelagiri hills. Invasion of Keedapattu village by the extremists left two dead and 27 injured. Ten cases were registered in 1979, and in the first half of 1980 their writ ran free in Tirupattur area with as many as 27 incidents reported.

The turning point was a sensational incident which took place on 6th of August 1980. Along with four constables Inspector Palaniswamy secured three suspected Naxalites from Yelagiri village during combing operations. While being brought to the station in a car one of the suspects, later identified as Sivalingam, took out a bomb and exploded it. The driver and a suspect, Chinnathamby, remained unhurt, Sivalingam escaped although he was injured. The Inspector, two constables and Naxalites Selvam, Rajappa and Perumal died.

The state government condoled the death of the policemen and announced substantial compensation. The Chief Minister Dr MGR himself attended the funeral along with the DGP and the Home Secretary and for the first time it was made clear that the government was behind the police and there was a marked change in its attitude which had led to severe demoralisation post Seeralan episode. Four additional police stations were opened, three in North Arcot and one in Dharmapuri. With solidarity declared, the police swung into action under the legendary leadership of Walter Davaram, the then DIG Vellore range. Concerted action by him and his team in Tirupattur area dealt a severe blow to the movement and virtually neutralised it. However, small groups such as TNRT continued to indulge in isolated incidents in the Vanniah belt. Most of the cases were detected and TN Police was able to contain their activities. The last major action was an encounter with an RYL (Radical Youth League) outfit in Dharmapuri district in 2004.

Since then the state has been more or less quiet on this front except some isolated incidents of apprehension of cadres like Alapakkam Murugesan and others for possession of explosives. A major recovery of arms component in Andhra Pradesh in August 2006 brought to light a new area of the problem. A consignment of indigenously prepared rocket launchers and hand grenade shells was recovered by AP Police from a godown of Kranti Transport in Vijaywada. Investigation revealed that such consignments were transported from Chennai by the same transporter. Our 'Q' branch immediately swung into action and located the small scale industry in Ambattur which had fabricated the components of the rocket launchers and hand grenades. The person, who had provided the design and placed the orders, was identified to be one Tech Madhu, a cadre of the PWG (People's War Group, CPM Maoist). He had married a cadremate Vasantha and the two were staying in a rented accommodation in Ambattur. Search of the premises yielded incriminating material linking the couple with the Maoist movement in Andhra. All the consignments were intended for the Maoists.

Excellent coordination was established between TN and AP Police and since the major part of the crime concerned Andhra Pradesh, the case was transferred to Andhra with the approval of the court. Though there was no activity directly affecting our state this case brought out the fact that Tamil Nadu was being utilised to source the extremist outfit in Andhra Pradesh. This was taken as an alarm bell and vigilance was stepped up.

Two small units had already been pressed into service in Dharmapuri and Krishnagiri districts not only for combing but also initiating development activities. Youngsters in the Naxalite prone villages were involved in sports, mobile library arranged for them and schemes worked out for organising trade training to help them secure employment in Hosur industrial area near Bangalore. Vigilance was extended to Vellore, Tiruvalluvar districts, prone to infiltration, being bordering districts. With the heat turned on the residual elements of the hitherto vulnerable areas they tried to regroup in the Southern districts, but were nabbed in time while trying to organise arms training in the foothills of Western Ghats just three kilometers away from Periakulam. The entire training material was seized.

A daring operation, the 'Q' branch ventured into, started after the interception of a mechanised boat belonging to LTTE on 13.2.07. The boat was intercepted by the Indian Coast Guard ship 'Ramadevi' while patrolling the stretch between India and Sri Lanka in Palk Strait. Four LTTE cadres and one Ramachandran of TN were on board. All of them were taken into custody by Coast Guard and brought to Chennai harbour where they were handed over to the state police. One AK-56 rifle with 124 rounds of ammunition, five hand grenades, one explosive filled jacket, eight barrels of chemical, a satellite phone and ration articles seized from the boat were also handed over. Even before we took up the case the Coast Guard officials went to town tomtoming their good work. Due to inept interrogation, wrong information got publicised that the boat would have struck the Cuddalore area had it not been intercepted. This triggered speculations in the media that LTTE was targeting Tamil Nadu. Our interrogation revealed that the boat coming from Iraiantheevu was heading to the high seas north of Jaffna, perhaps to escort a ship load of arms and ammunition coming from the Far East for use by LTTE against the Sri Lankan army. Deprived of the escort, the consignment could not secure its passage to the destination and was learnt to have been destroyed by the Sri Lankan Navy. The LTTE boat was intercepted by the Coast Guard in the Indian waters while trying to evade surveillance by the Sri Lankan Navy.

Interrogation of the LTTE cadres revealed that more explosives were concealed inside the fibre glass plates on both sides and the front portion of the boat which could be detonated to cause havoc. The material would cause severe damage to the harbour and destroy the ships berthed nearby. Hence, it was decided to explode the boat in the high seas so as to neutralise any risk to the harbour and the ships. Court orders were obtained accordingly.

A very risky venture was undertaken by the 'Q' branch led by AK Viswanathan, DIG and a team consisting of the Commandant Coast Guard, central and state intelligence officials boarded a Coast Guard ship which towed the explosives laden boat about 20 nautical miles east of Chennai. The daredevils of our bomb disposal squad got into the boat and laid the fuse wire. The other officials waited with baited breath as the desperadoes escaped to safety in a small Coast Guard boat after lighting the fuse wire. The LTTE boat was blown into smithereens and the smoke rose upto 200 ft in the sky. The entire sequence was video recorded.

In the office, I could hardly concentrate on my work as anxiety had gripped me. The tension ended finally at about 11.30 hours when Nanjil Kumaran, ADGP, Intelligence walked in with a smiling face.

Although no evidence was forthcoming to indicate any direct activity of the LTTE in Tamil Nadu during these years, it was common knowledge that the organisation was depending on sympathisers from the mainland for supply of food, medicines and even hardware such as steel ball bearings and aluminium ingots used in the manufacture of ammunition, propellants and casing material. The entire coastal security group and the local police of the coastal districts were pressed into service for prevention of smuggling. A fair degree of success was achieved and seizures effected. However, an area of persistent concern that kept on haunting the police and the state government, emanated from our fishermen straying into Sri Lankan waters controlled by the LTTE, in search of better catch of fish. Many instances of our fishermen going missing were reported and even murderous attacks came to light. Many people believed that these attacks were perpetrated by the Sri Lankan Navy, but the following sequence of events brought to light the involvement of the LTTE.

In the first week of March 2007, ten fishermen from Colachel, Kanyakumari district, along with another one from Tuticorin ventured into the sea in a boat 'Sri Krishna' driven by one Simon from Kerala, who also happened to be a mechanic. Since they did not return till 20.3.07, a case of 'man was missing' was registered at Kavanadu police station in Kerala. The following were the missing fishermen – Kingsley, Clements, Thathayur, Deepak, Joseph Thathayur, James, Jesudasan, Albert, Franklin, Prabhu, and Simon.

While frantic efforts continued to ascetain the whereabouts of the missing fishermen another incident took place on 29.3.07. Nine fishermen fishing in Indian waters were attacked by some unknown persons who came in two boats. One of them was 'Maria' and those travelling in it opened fire and killed five of the Indian fishermen. The remaining four returned home and on their report a case was registered in Nitravilai police station, Kanyakumari.

The said 'Maria' boat had an engine failure during a subsequent trip on 12.4.07 and was seized by Indian Coast Guard with six Sri Lankan Tamils and six Indian fishermen from Kanyakumari on board. Investigation by 'Q' branch revealed that the six Sri Lankans were, in fact, Sea Tigers of LTTE and were deployed to smuggle explosives from Maldives area to their camp at Kokkupadayan in Sri Lanka. They were Robin, Bonypas, Ravi Kumar, Arul Gunanadasan, Arul, an Selvakumar. The same group turned out to be the killers of the five fishermen in the incident dated 29.3.07. It transpired that the Indian group could not affect a good catch and approached the occupants of Maria to share their catch. On being refused by the Sri Lankans, they attempted to grab the load forcefully. The load was, in fact, a cache of explosives and hence the provocation. The mystery of the twelve missing fishermen was also solved as the arrested tigers 1. Robin, 2. Bonypas, 3. Ravi Kumar, 4. Arul Gunasekharan, 5. Arul, 6. Selva Kumar admitted the abduction of these persons. The captives were kept at an island near Mannar and subsequently moved from place to place in Sri Lanka. The boat 'Sri Krishna' along with Simon, the driver-cum-mechanic, was utilised by LTTE for trans-shipment of arms and ammunition. It was learnt later that on 17.5.07 the boat was fired upon by the Maldivian defence forces in its territorial waters. The boat went up in flames and sank. Simon, who was taken in custody, was released by the Maldivian Government and reached Trivandrum on 4.7.07.

Following the apprehension of the six Sea Tigers on 20.4.07 communication was established with the captors of the twelve Indian fishermen and request routed through these Tigers for their early release. In the meantime, the story had broken out in the national and international media. The Sea Tigers took these eleven fishermen to sea on 17.5.07 and handed them over to Indian fishermen. They reached Rameshwaram on 18.5.07 and Chennai the next day. They appeared before the Chief Minister and narrated their tales of woe. The CM was kind enough to hand over Rs 10,000 per head as immediate relief. Subsequently, the fishermen were grilled by the media to pick holes in their story with a view to score out the involvement of LTTE. But the victims stuck to their guns and their narration was too cogent to evoke any suspicion.

The truthful account of the events was contested by the sympathisers of LTTE including a section of the media. A website of the banned organisation carried a vitriolic broadside on the Tamil Nadu police, particularly the police chief (the author).

Apart from some of the major incidents narrated above there was a host of events which had grave potential for generating law and order problems, but we have to rest content describing them as 'passed off peacefully'. "When something untoward takes place it becomes news. Its absence does not attract any attention. People have no idea how much effort goes behind ensuring the event passing off peacefully. The temple car festival at Kanda Devi, Sivagangai district, was one such event. There was a long standing dispute between Ambalakarars and Adi Dravidas about participating in the car festival. The anxiety was of such dimension that even the CM felt concerned. High level meetings were held a month prior to the event and the *bandobast* scheme discussed threadbare. The ADGP law and order, was deputed to personally supervise the *bandobast*. I kept monitoring the situation throughout the day. Finally, when I communicated to the CM of the incident-free conclusion of the festival, his sigh of relief was easily discernible.

There were events galore where caste-based passions ruled the roost and the slightest friction could wreak havoc on public peace. These included the car festival at Sakkottai, Sivagangai district, martyrs day at Unjanai, in memory of Adi Dravidas killed during a caste clash in Sivagangai district in 1979, martyrs day at Melavalavu, Madurai district, and Thevar Jayanti celebrations which required meticulous and elaborate *bandobast* throughout Ramnad and Sivagangai districts. *Vinayakar Chaturthi* celebrations presented a mega challenge to the police especially during the immersion processions. In several places there was strong disagreement between Hindus and Muslims on the route to be followed. Dindigul, Muthupettai, Tiruvarur district and Egmore were the places where serious problems were anticipated, but nothing untoward happened.

Fifteen months passed like fifteen days and 31st of August 2007 arrived like a bolt. It was time to go home. When I took leave of the CM it was with a sense of satisfaction of having given proper direction to the force in improving its image and upholding human rights at any cost. In recognition of my efforts, in this direction the Government awarded me the Chief Minister's medal for 'Excellence in Public Service'.

As I drove out of Rajaratnam stadium after the farewell parade, I dreamt of the future. The rich traditions of Tamil Nadu police and its professional competence will keep its flag flying and lead the caravan through the sands of time.

Chapter – 23

Crusade Against Corruption
A Losing Battle

One of the earliest instances of corruption has been described in the Biblical history, namely the story of Adam and Eve. The couple was forbidden by the Lord, Who created them, from eating the apple found in Eden, the celestial garden. Enticed by Satan they violated the instruction and consumed the forbidden fruit, thereby committing a sin by breaking the rule of law. In today's parlance, they indulged in corruption. Satan is the one who corrupted them. The cardinal principle the violation of which amounts to corruption is "Not to Appease or Gratify Oneself against the Rule of Law".

Chemistry of Corruption—"Power corrupts. Absolute power corrupts absolutely. Power begets corruption. Corruption in turn breeds power". Corruption has three major ingredients—Wine, Women and Wealth, that is, WWW popularly enunciated.

Applying the coordinates of modern day life corruption can be said to be the sum total of all successful efforts by individuals or groups of individuals to corner the assets of the nation. In the process, the nation is denied the use of these assets for its growth. This leads to lack of development and consequently the nation continues to be weak.

For corruption to take place, a public servant must be endowed with some authority and there should be abuse of such authority which would cause pecuniary gain to such public servant or to any other person and corresponding loss to the government. This could be applicable to private sector, *mutatis mutandis.* Corruption, as stated in the case of public servants is covered under Section 13(1)d of the Prevention of Corruption Act 1988. The broad anti-corruption strategy as adopted in our country is three pronged. Efforts are made to get people at the cutting edge level trapped (caught red handed) and the higher categories of public servants targeted for accumulation of assets disproportionate to their known sources of income. A trap is the culmination of a particular instance of abuse of authority. Assets are acquired from the money earned through multiple instances of abuse of authority. Category of cases grossly outnumbering traps and asset cases are those relating to abuse of authority alone.

Tackling of corruption is linked with the concept of secret services. This is known in ancient civilizations like Egypt, Babylon, Greece and China and referred to as the second oldest profession. Over the years the concept of vigilance and the organisations charged with this responsibility have grown substantially but the first time it got codified was by Kautilya only. While the physical security of the country was the prime concern at that time now the economic security is equally important. Corruption paves the way for undermining the economy. This cancerous malady has been an ever growing phenomenon.

The words Integrity and Honesty are antithesis of this dreadful disease. The concept of even these virtues has been diluted with the passage of time. Earlier even the private use of official vehicles/telephones was taboo. Now, this malpractice has been taken for granted and not frowned upon provided the officer is otherwise honest. The dilution started in 1985 with the government permitting officers of and above the rank of Joint Secretary to use government vehicles for coming to office and back. Officers down below picked up the cue and started asserting their claim. It was not possible for the government to come down with a heavy hand since the privilege granted to Joint Secretaries and above was clearly discriminatory. Now, officers of the rank of SPs and above in local police have more than one vehicle at their command. Some officers even earmark vehicles exclusively for their families.

When EL Stracy was the Chief of TN Police he ordered sharing of vehicles by officers coming to the same function. The COP Madras used to be seen travelling with two Deputy Commissioners of Police in the same vehicle. I remember a situation in 1977 when various range DIGs had assembled at Vellore on the eve of the Inter Range Games Meet. These officers had gathered at the SPs bungalow when information was received that Mr Stracy had arrived at the stadium. Immediately, the officers started getting into their respective vehicles to proceed to the stadium. A thoughtful officer, Mr Sripal, DIG Training, suddenly remembered the instruction of the IGP and cautioned his colleagues. Quietly the officers started getting out and regrouping themselves ensuring that the number of vehicles did not exceed one per three officers.

When my ASP had to proceed to Madurai for court work, he made the mistake of taking his official jeep. Mr Stracy happened to be camping at Madurai that day. He was rather pleased when the ASP called on him. He even invited the young officer for lunch. However, the ASP was shocked to find a memo on his return to Tirunelveli. In fact, as Superintendent of Police, Tirunelveli I had received the original to call for the explanation of the ASP for wasting money on petrol when the journey (154 km×2) could have been performed economically by public transport. Thus the fuel cost was recovered from the ASP.

The same rigidity was seen in the private use of official telephones. Trunk call register had to be maintained by each officer to distinguish between official and private calls. As Superintendent of Police, Tirunelveli I had to submit a factual report to the IGP on the private calls made by a predecessor. The latter requested me to give some time to enable him remit the amount so that the fact of payment could be included in the report. I obliged the officer in good faith and received a memo from the Chief for delaying the report. The IGP further observed that the charges were remitted only after the enquiry was ordered. Thus, the strategy did not help the officer either as the Chief gave him a damaging entry in the annual confidential report.

Another anecdote remembered about the same police chief concerns an ASP, who irritated by the harassment meted out by his SP, rang up IGP in sheer desperation and wanted to know about his promotion. Irked by the indiscreet behaviour of the ASP he angrily retorted, "That's none of your business. You will keep the phone down and remit the trunk call charges".

There is hardly any walk of life unaffected by this dreadful disease today. The common man experiences it at the cutting edge level – for getting community certificate, reservation in trains, installation or restoration of telephone connections, getting electricity connection, gratifying the traffic cop to escape challans, etc. The elite are not averse to following the short cut when it comes to them. Otherwise they are in the habit of condemning the malpractice vociferously in drawing rooms and public platforms. Bribe money plays a big role in the corporate sector, especially in the procurement of goods and services. There is hardly any purchase in which there is no kickback. Now the vendors camouflage this as "service charges". Some leave the extra amount to be accounted for in sub-contracts. The mega deals of questionable character such as purchase of Jaguar fighters, HDW submarines, Bofors, Barrack missiles and several banking scams, etc are common knowledge. Middlemen play an important role in such transactions.

Prior to the Second World War corruption was perhaps of manageable dimensions and did not warrant extraordinary attention. The war department witnessed massive purchases for the army and other combat units. These transactions had tremendous potential for corruption by unscrupulous contractors in collusion with defence personnel. Hence, the Government of India had to take serious note which led to the creation of Special Police Establishment, which in turn gave birth to the CBI. As can be seen the lack of integrity in public procurement only paved the way for creating an effective body armed with statutory powers to fight corruption. Thus, the importance of integrity in public procurement.

A study conducted by the Organisation of Economic Cooperation and Developing Countries (OECD) revealed that in the European Union public procurement in 2002 alone aggregated to 1.5 trillion euros and in OECD member countries, public procurement accounted for as much as 15 per cent of the Gross Domestic Product (GDP). Hence, one can imagine how much money can be saved by plugging the loopholes in the procurement system and neutralising the bribery involved. Corruption thrives in secrecy. Hence, transparency and accountability are the key factors in promoting integrity in public procurement. Conversely, the lack of these traits poses a grave threat to integrity in the public sector.

Reverting back to the privilege showered upon the ruling class, namely, Joint Secretary and above in the matter of private use of official transport, it is no wonder that the same class of people was granted another favour, this one far more important and having far reaching consequences. I am referring to the oft discussed and hotly debated "Single directive" a red rag to CBI. Ironically, this order was also issued the same year by the Congress Government. The directive accords protection to officers of and above the rank of Joint Secretary before commencing any enquiry or investigation. As per the directive, prior permission of the Government is required before taking up any preliminary inquiry or regular case against an officer of the above category. Already protection is available against malicious prosecution through Section 19 of Prevention of Corruption Act and Section 197 CrPC. What was the need for another protection? If a serious allegation is guillotined even before verifying the complaint how could the society know the truth? Further, what is the justification in arming only the privileged section of the bureaucracy with this protection leaving the lesser mortals (Deputy Secretary and below) to fend for themselves? Perhaps the consideration was that the privileged class formed the decision-making level and would require moral support of the Government in all the flipflops carried out to implement the desires of the political hierarchy who would like to remain in the background.

The order was not only discriminatory, but unconstitutional as well. When the commission of a cognisable offence is revealed, the police (that includes CBI also) have no other option but to register a case. No wonder the Supreme Court struck it down. The mandarins in the North Block circumvented this obstacle by putting it on a statutory footing as a part of the CVC Act. Any Government appears to enjoy exercising this control. Of course, they are helpless when the High Court or Supreme Court orders an investigation by CBI.

The attitudinal change in the mind of the Government with the passage of time is inexplicable. In 1973, following a CBI case against an IAS officer a delegation of officers called on the Home Secretary LP Singh. While torpedoing the suggestion of making it mandatory to obtain approval of the Government before registering a case against an All India Service officer, the Home Secretary minuted, "This would lead to emasculation of CBI".

It is strange that the same clan somersaulted from this stance and went headlong to secure the discriminatory protection for their fraternity. Even if a case is permitted to be registered, invariably the suspect officer is able to get wind of it and is in a position to work out measures that would render the consequent searches futile. This is a great impediment for the investigating agency since the success of the investigation often depends upon the outcome of a successful search. Thus, the single directive is more of an obstacle in the administration of justice. The authority granted to the Government may be misused to protect a guilty official or deny protection to an innocent bureaucrat if he/she is not toeing the line.

In this connection, I recall a proposal initiated by CBI Bangalore for registering a case against the Managing Director of Hindustan Aeronautics Limited for registering a case on charges of abuse of authority in the purchase of avionic accessories. The officer being a board level employee, permission of the department of defence production was required. The proposal was sent with the approval of the director CBI. Apparently, the suspect officer enjoyed support of the government and queries were raised. When the director reiterated his stand the secretary desired the matter to be discussed with a senior officer. Either SP Bangalore or any of his superior officers should have been deputed for the purpose, but the director sent an officer from the headquarter who had not dealt with the case. After discussion he endorsed the views of the secretary and the director agreed to close the matter. Thus no case could be registered and the suspect officer soon got elevated to the post of Chairman. The poor chief vigilance officer, a senior IPS officer of impeccable integrity, who had shared the basic information with CBI, had to leave the job and go back to his state cadre.

Corruption is a universal phenomenon as stated by Prime Minister Indira Gandhi. Prime Minister Deve Gowda was also right when he posed the question, "Is there any country which is not corrupt"? while addressing a CBI conference. It is only a variation in the degree of corruption. It is a sad reality that our country figures very low in the transparency index, or high on the corruption index.

Although the Indian Penal Code did contain a chapter on corruption, Sections 161 to 169, relating to public servants effective use of the same was not discernible. Taking serious note of the massive misappropriation of war funds by contractors in connivance with defence officials the Government of India created a Special Police Cell in the war department with HQ at Lahore in 1941. In 1946, Delhi Special Police Establishment Act was brought in force and HQ shifted to Delhi, bringing the supervision under the Home Ministry. The DSPE did not have the authority to investigate cases in states without their concurrence. Initially, there was no difficulty on this score since the same party (Congress) was ruling at the Centre as well as the States. The scenario changed in 1967, leading to problems in obtaining consent of the concerned states under Section 6 of the Act.

A committee on prevention of corruption set up in 1962 under the chairmanship of Mr Santhanam, Member of Parliament came out with a broad spectrum of recommendations for fighting corruption. One of the major suggestions was the establishment of a Premier Central Investigating Agency. Thus, DSPE blossomed into the present Central Bureau of Investigation.

Instead of passing an Act to arm the CBI with powers to investigate corruption at all levels the then Government did not do so for reasons best known to it and created CBI only through a resolution, leaving the Premier agency to continue to function under the DSPE Act with its limitations. The subsequent Governments also failed on this score. I witnessed an instance of the helplessness of CBI while supervising a case handled by a Central Investigating Unit. Two cases were referred by the Government of Manipur for investigation by CBI when the state was under President's rule. These related to diversion and misappropriation of edible oil intended for public distribution. The oil was allocated to the state by the Government of India and imported through the State Trading Corporation. Calcutta was the port of entry and the stock was to be lifted by authorised agents of the Manipur Government and transported for public distribution. Instead it was diverted and sold in black market at Calcutta. This was revealed by the seizure of large quantities of the oil by the Calcutta police. The FIRs contained names of VIPs including the concerned minister.

Investigation began in right earnest and in the initial stage itself the likelihood of an important role being played by the Chief Minister surfaced. Within a few days of the registration, President's rule was revoked and a popular Government sworn in. Ironically, the same Chief Minister was chosen to head the ministry. The case was certainly an embarrassment for the Government of the day. In the midst of the investigation I received a query from CBI head office about the evidence against the Chief Minister. I replied that though investigation was at the initial stage the evidence collected till that time indicated the possibility of the involvement of the Chief Minister. The reply would have triggered a brain storming exercise to find out a way of aborting the investigation. This did not take long.

After all what were the mandarins in North Block meant for? Soon, the Manipur Government withdrew its consent under Section 6 of DSPE Act which gives licence to CBI to function in that state. The CBI head office did not lose a day to hammer home its decision that since we do not exist in Manipur, there is no other option but to file a closure report in the court. The investigating officer was virtually chased to fly down to Imphal along with trunk loads of documents seized during investigation only to be returned to the government of Manipur. The particular special judge was rather difficult to deal with. He experienced the political game and it became very difficult to convince him about our helpless position. Finally, he agreed to close the case which involved crores of public money and deprived the common man of (ration card holders) his due. Ultimately, CBI had to cut a sorry figure. It is a different matter that the legal position has changed somewhat now, thanks to the Supreme Court which has ruled that sanction once given cannot be withdrawn.

The scope of corruption became very much wider after the nationalisation of banks and insurance companies as well as the mushrooming growth of the public sector. 1977 saw a change of guard at the centre, with Janata Party sweeping the polls. The CBI, which was hijacked to the PMO during emergency, was brought back to MHA. The new government entrusted cases concerning the former Prime Minister and secretaries to the government and compelled the CBI to contravene its own instructions enshrined in its manual regarding arrests and incarcerated many VIPs of the previous day including the former Prime Minister Indira Gandhi. This was the starting point for misuse of the agency by successive governments in power to harass its adversaries.

A legal weapon coming in extremely handy for politicians in power is the authority to accord sanction for prosecution.

While narrating my last innings in CBI, I had referred to the Taj Corridor case. The investigation of this case was subjected to intense scrutiny. As per the culture of collective decision followed in CBI, a battery of officers gave their assessment of the evidence after the report of investigation was submitted by the IO. These included the senior public prosecutor, the SP, deputy legal advisor, the DIG, additional legal advisor, joint director, director of prosecution and the additional director (the author). Except the senior PP and the director of prosecution all others recommended prosecution. The Director referred the matter to the Attorney General for opinion. The latter went with the minority view that it was not a case fit for prosecution. Based on his opinion, Director ordered closure of the case.

Thereafter, the CBI's decision to close the case, with departmental action against a few officials, was hotly contested and agitated before the Supreme Court. The latter obtained the opinion of the Central Vigilance Commission also and ordered action to be taken as proposed by the SP.

In compliance of this order the investigating officer filed a chargesheet in the special court. The latter pointed out that sanction for prosecution was required. His Excellency, the Governor of Uttar Pradesh was requested to accord sanction. The Governor, TV Rajeswar, a former Director of Intelligence Bureau, however, had no dilemma. He was clear that the case did not warrant prosecution of Mayawati, the Chief Minister and Nasimuddin Siddique, Minister although the Apex Court had put its seal on the proposed line of action. It was heard in the corridors of power that those were the days when an alliance was being chalked out between Congress and Bahujan Samaj Party.

Whether the talks between the two political parties had any bearing on the response of the Governor is a matter of academic interest only. The fact remains that a legal provision was misused to protect a wrong doer. One feels rather anguished to digest how a sum of Rs 17 crore went out of the treasury without obtaining any benefit to the tax payer. To boot, think of the demoralisation of the investigators who left no stone unturned in arriving at the truth.

In 1996 an interesting issue came up before the High Court of Madras. The Collector Madurai had given a contract to a defunct Industrial Cooperative Society for construction of 70 cremation sheds under the Jawahar Rozgar Yojna at a cost of Rs 30 thousand each. Fifty per cent advance was already given. Before making the balance payment the Additional Collector, Umashankar IAS, raised objections since inspection revealed the work to be of sub-standard. This resulted in some administrative action against the Additional Collector. He in turn, went to the High Court. The High Court came down heavily on the administration and ordered a CBI investigation on the projects undertaken throughout the state. Accordingly 19 cases were registered, each covering one revenue district. Altogether about two thousand sheds were put up.

Investigation revealed that it was a state-level conspiracy at macro level and also a conspiracy at district level (micro). The deliberations started with Chengalpattu district where a type design of the cremation shed was furnished by a contractor. The collector, not only awarded the work, but also suggested its adoption in other districts. The contractor bagged the order by furnishing his quotation on the letterhead of an Industrial Cooperative Society which was defunct.

At government level several Industrial Cooperative Societies were identified and an order issued to all collectors to issue work order to anyone of those societies for fabrication of cremation sheds under the JRY scheme. Most of the collectors awarded the work in compliance of the GO while six of them started the work even before the receipt of the GO. These officers along with the contractor and other subordinates were identified for prosecution. The macro level conspirators included Selvaganapathy, the Minister for Local Administration, JT Acharyulu IAS, Secretary Rural Development and Sathiamurthy, IAS, Director Rural Development. It was revealed that cremation sheds were not listed in the JRY manual and employment of contractors or intermediaries was prohibited. Work had to be completed by local people only. The same contractor happened to bag all the orders by submitting the offer on the letterhead of the societies. All these societies were defunct and all the sheds were found to be sub-standard.

Officials of seven districts were recommended to be prosecuted. State level officers figured in all such cases. Departmental action was suggested against others. In respect of the mother case (Madurai district) both the Central and the State Governments accorded sanction for prosecution and the case stands chargesheeted. Trouble started when the Government of India was approached to accord sanction in respect of the Collectors of Chengalpattu and Pudukottai districts. By that time the BJP had come to power at Delhi. An important functionary of the party hailing from Andhra Pradesh took up the cause of these officers as both were from Andhra. The Department of Personnel raised several queries and each one of them was replied convincingly.

Even when the issue was pending at Delhi with the Department of Personnel, the DMK lost the election in Tamil Nadu and AIADMK took over. The latter spread its canopy over the bureaucracy. When I went to pay a courtesy call on the new Chief Secretary, he immediately queried, "You have come for those sanctions? We are not going to give them. The collectors have only obeyed the Government instructions. Even I would have done the same."I humbly submitted that this was only a courtesy call. However, since the Chief Secretary had raised the issue, I clarified that only those collectors who had issued the work order even before the issue of the GO were being sought to be proceeded against.

Shortly thereafter, the midnight drama involving the arrest of the former CM Dr Karunanidhi took place for his alleged roll in the fly-over scam. The infuriated DMK, who were a part of the NDA Government, were seething to take revenge. It did not take long to ascertain that the complainant was JT Acharyulu, Special officer Chennai Corporation. The same person figured as accused number two in all the cremation shed cases. Some adversary tipped off the NDA Government that sanction for prosecution was awaited in three cases. The same Government which was dragging its feet in the main cases, those pertaining to Chengalpattu and Pudukottai suddenly jumped into action on the cases referred to. I was summoned to Delhi and instructed to contact the acting Director PC Sharma on arrival. When I contacted him he asked me to wait in the CBI guest house. Within half an hour he came over and handed over a packet containing sanction orders in the cases relating to Acharyulu and instructed me to file chargesheet the next day.

I took the early morning flight back to Chennai and straightaway commenced operation "chargesheet". Further instructions were received to forward the accused to the court in custody. In other words Acharyulu had to be arrested before filing the chargesheet. I pointed out to PC Sharma that the list of accused included a minister in the AIADMK cabinet and his arrest was fraught with repercussions. He quickly grasped the problem and asked me to wait till further orders. Perhaps he briefed the PMO. Luckily sanity prevailed and the idea of arresting Acharyulu was dropped. Nevertheless, chargesheet was filed at the end of the day. Of course, the retaliatory action of putting Acharyulu behind bars, as his action had led to the mid-night arrest of the DMK leader, had to be put in the cold storage.

In none of the remaining cases CBI could lay chargesheet as sanction was denied by the State Government. This set of cases, known as "Cremation shed scam" ultimately landed in the crematorium, but not before exposing the vulnerability of the investigation due to the improper use of the provision for sanction. On principle this power need to be there only to protect honest public servants for acts done in good faith. Misuse of the authority with a view to shield the dishonest creed and for malafide actions deserves to be condemned. Section 19 PC Act and 197 CrPC should be amended to include – "If sanction is denied for unconvincing reasons, the court should be enabled to take cognizance, sans sanction, if it is convinced, after perusing the case records, that there is a prima facie case". The cremation shed scam also demonstrates how the destiny of a public servant swings with the change in Governments. Heroes become villains and villain's heroes. While the accused collectors earned their elevation in due course, the whistle blower came to grief.

Out of all cases chargesheeted, a few got discharged in the beginning stage itself, a sizeable number got convicted while the remaining ended into acquittal. As per the procedure followed in the CBI the judgment is studied by the prosecutor who offers his comments on the suitability of filing appeal against acquittal/inadequate sentence or revision against the order of discharge. The line of action proposed is further examined up the hierarchy and final decision taken by the Director CBI. The drill assumes great importance in cases concerning VIPs and usually appeal is filed when there is a slightest infirmity in the judgment. One case in which the supervisory officers defaulted and decided against filing an appeal contrary to the strong recommendations of the IO is the Southern Petrochemial Industrial Corporation (SPIC) case involving the CM of Tamil Nadu, Secretary, Industries and AC Muthiah, Vice Chairman of SPIC. This case originated from a writ petition filed by Dr Subramaniam Swamy.

SPIC was a joint venture enterprise, the TN Government holding 26 per cent of the share capital through Tamil Nadu Industrial Development Corporation (TIDCO) whereas MA Chidambaram and AC Muthiah held 25 per cent. As per the Articles of Association of SPIC the board was competent to elect its chairman and it chose MA Chidambaram. In 1989 when DMK Government came to power it pointed out that as per joint venture norms the Chairman should be the nominee of the Government. Although Miss Jayalalithaa allowed the same arrangement to continue even after she had become the CM, she reverted back to the old position in 1992 and the chairmanship was handed back to MA Chidambaram. This was a clear favour towards the business tycoon.

In 1991 SPIC came up with its rights issue in the form of zero interest fully convertible bonds. Each bond was to consist of 25 shares at the rate of Rs 25 per share. Although TIDCO decided to invest in the scheme and requested the Government to sanction Rs 12.37 crore as "Ways and means advance" the Government decided to renounce its rights with respect to its existing 88.4 lakh shares equivalent to 1,76,800 bonds. To work out the flow of funds TIDCO suggested two approaches, one is economic time formula and other is go by the market value.

Since the bonds were being traded in the market at Rs 2000 per bond the following options were available with the Government.

Sell the bonds at market rate which would have fetched the Government Rs 35.36 crore. Option (1) would have netted Rs 16.20 crore. However, the Government directed TIDCO to consider the loss in interest that SPIC would suffer since the bonds were to accumulate no interest till they qualify for conversion into actual shares which is after 18 months. Accordingly the price of 176800 bonds was worked out to Rs 12.37 crore. Thus there was a minimum loss of 3.83 crore to TIDCO for which the accused were responsible.

It was an open and shut case, a glaring example of abuse of authority and should have been taken for appeal. The culture of collective decision notwithstanding sometimes the decision-making gets influenced by the recommendations of the senior officers. In the instant case, the IO K Raghottaman (one of the best I have come across) had a thorough grip over the case, but his services were not utilised at the trial stage. Needless to say his views were not heard when he made out a solid case for appeal. Thus, justice was stopped from reaching its final destination.

In spite of continuing flops I believe CBI can still regain its lost glory by strictly following its impressive motto "Industry, Impartiality, Integrity" and the positive message flying around with the National Emblem—"Truth Alone Triumphs".

Index

Some of our learned Authors

General S Padmanabhan; General VP Malik; Air Chief Marshal Fali Homi Major; Admiral Vishnu Bhagwat; Admiral Nirmal Verma; Admiral Arun Prakash; Vice Admiral Vijay Shankar; Lt Gen Arjun Ray; Dr A Sivathanu Pillai DRDO; Parvez Dewan IAS; Dhirendra Singh IAS; Kalyan Ray IAS; Sangeeta Goel IAS; HN Das IAS; Dr Surender Ghonkrokta IAS; Falguni Rajkumar IAS; G Sundaram IAS; PS Bhatnagar IAS; N Vittal IAS; PK Agrawal IAS; Sudhir S Baloeria IAS; NS Sisodia IAS; Dhirendra Singh IAS; Dr Yogendra Narain IPS; JK Bagchi IAS; TSR Subramanian IAS; Prakash Singh IPS; DC Nath IPS; Ajit Doval IPS; SP Mathur IPS; MK Dhar IPS; SK Datta IPS; HS Swan IPS; BR Lall IPS; PC Dogra IPS; DC Pathak IPS; ML Kumawat IPS; Dr. S Subramanian IPS; RK Ohri IPS; RB Sreekumar IPS; Kalyan K Mitra IPS; RS Gupta IPS; K Koshy IPS; Kuldeep Khoda IPS; Ajay Kashyap IPS; Dr N Dilip Kumar IPS; Dr Nazrul Islam IPS; Dr DV Guruprasad IPS; AP Maheshwari IPS; Loknath Behera IPS; Dr NC Asthana IPS; PM Nair IPS; Dr Sundari Nanda IPS; Keshav Kumar IPS; Dr Prateep V Philip IPS; Muktesh Chander IPS; Dr PS Pasricha IPS; VK Agarwal IRS; Virendra Gupta IFS; Lt Gen SK Sinha; Lt Gen Raj Kadyan; Lt Gen Mukesh Sabharwal; Lt Gen HB Kala; Lt Gen PC Katoch; Lt Gen Gautam Banerjee; Lt Gen Ashok Kapur; Vice Admiral Suresh Bangara; Lt Gen CK Kapur; Lt Gen NS Narahari; Lt Gen Chandra Shekhar; Lt Gen ML Chibber; Lt Gen Ashok Joshi; Lt Gen DB Shekatkar; Lt Gen SRR Aiyengar; Lt Gen Utpal Bhattacharyya; Lt Gen Kamal Davar; Lt Gen Amitav Mukherji; Maj Gen Nilendra Kumar; Maj Gen Vinod Saighal; Maj Gen VK Singh; Maj Gen Anjan Mukherjee; Maj Gen Raj Mehta; Maj Gen Samay Ram; Maj Gen Y Behl; Maj Gen GD Bakshi; Gen Deepak Kapoor; Air Marshal SR Deshpande; Air Marshal RC Bajpai; Air Chief Marshal PV Naik; Air Vice Marshal AK Tiwary; Air Cmde (Dr) CN Ghosh; Ambassador Kishan S Rana IFS; Cmde Ranjit B Rai; Capt (IN) Alok Bansal; VK Singal IRS; Sudha Raman; Brig Yash Mohan; Brig Trigunesh Mukherjee; Brig. MS Patial; Col PK Gautam; Col Arun Jha; Col MS Jaswal; Col Anil Shorey; Lt Col Anil Bhatt; Dr Harsh Vardhan; Ratan Sharda, Sudhakar Raje; Dr RK Tiwari; Anuj Dhar, Journalist; Ranjit Kumar, Journalist; SK Vikram; Gopal Chowdhuri; Dr Pramod Sharma; Swati Sharma, etc.

Other Valuable Books of Related Interest

Conspiracy to Kill Rajiv Gandhi: From CBI Files, by K Ragothaman (Former SP - CBI)

India's Spy Agencies: Shaken not Stirred, by Sunil S Parihar

Amazing Ladakh: Travel, trckking, religion, culture, wildlife almost everything about Leh-Kargil-Zanskar-Siachen, by Parvez Dewan, IAS

Heroes of North East India, by Sumitra Mukherjee

The 21st Century Army: Strategies for Future, by Lt Gen Gautam Banerjee, PVSM, AVSM, YSM

Jungle Warfare: An Ultimate Handbook by Dr NC Asthana, IPS

Ultimate Handbook of Urban Warfare by Dr NC Asthana, IPS

Army Leadership, by Department of Army, US

Counter Insurgency Guide, by Bureau of Political-Military Affairs, US

Lens and the Guerrilla: Insurgency in India's Northeast, by Rajeev Bhattacharya **(fully Illustrated)**

Intelligence Tradecraft: Secrets of Spy Warfare, by MK Dhar (former Joint Director, IB)

Manas Police & Security Yearbook 2010-2011 (fully Illustrated) by Ajit Doval IPS, BR Lall, IPS and other Top Cops.

Manas Defence Year Book 2010-2011 (Fully Illustrated) by General S Padmanabhan and Lt Gen S Pattabhiraman

CBI Top-Cop Recalls by SK Dutta, IPS (Former Director – CBI)

Pakistan's Intelligence by Sudhakar Raje (Ex-Indian Diplomat)

Who Runs Police? Secrets of a Top Cop by HS Swan, IPS (Ex-DGP, Haryana)

Is It Police? Confessions of a Top Cop by Vinay Kumar Singh, IPS

Police and Naxalism: Strategies for Solutions by ML Kumawat, IPS, Nazrul Islam, IPS and others

Common Man's Guide to Police & Criminal Laws by Dr DV Guruprasad, IPS (DG – Karnataka Police)

Rainbow People: Reinventing Northeast India by Falguni Rajkumar, IAS (Former Sec NEC)

Industrial Security: Management & Strategies by DC Nath, IPS & Capt SB Tyagi

Intelligence, Security & Asymmetric Warfare by Dhirendra Singh, IAS and Lt Gen DB Shekatkar

Intelligence for Management by DC Pathak, IPS (Former Dir-Intelligence Bureau)

Inside IB and RAW: The Rolling Stone that Gathered Moss by K Sankaran Nair, IPS (Former Head: Research and Analysis Wing (RAW)

Intelligence: Corporate Success and Vigilance by D C Pathak, IPS (Ex Chief – IB)

The Undisclosed Punjab: India Besieged by Terror by Birbal Nath, IPS (Former DGP, Punjab)

The Folds of Insurgency by AP Maheshwari, IPS

Who Owns CBI? The Naked Truth by BR Lall, IPS (Former: Joint Director, CBI)

Saga of Civil Services by Dr Yogendra Narain, IAS (Former Defence Secretary)

Open Secrets: India's Intelligence Unveiled by M K Dhar, IPS

Security Manual by P Benjamin

SPYMASTER: My Life in the CIA by Ted Shackley

VIP Security: What You Need to know by Kanchan Sinha

Armed Forces Tribunal by Dr UC Jha

Beyond North East: Insurgency-History-Development by HN Das (Former Chief Secretary, Assam)

Why Bureaucracy Fails by Kalyan Ray, IAS

WMD Terrorism: Strategy for Consequences Management by Brig MS Patial

Intelligence Manual by Department of Defence, USA

The ISI Game Plan by Brig Yash Mohan, VSM

Terror, Insurgency and the State: Ending Protracted Conflicts by Marianne Heiberg etc.

Operation Triple X: An Indian Spy-Run in Pakistan A Novel by MK Dhar, IPS

Naxalism: Causes and Cure by PK Agrawal, IAS

Legal Safeguards for Defence Personnel by Air Cmde. Ranvir Kumar (Former Judge Advocate General)

Reforming Intelligence Agencies: Pakistan's Transitional Democracy by Frederic Grare

Combating Terrorism: Strategies of Ten Countries by Yonah Alexander

Strategies in Defence and Intelligence by Lt Gen S Pattabhiraman & MK Dhar, IPS

Sports, Games and Adventure Sports by Air Cmde (Dr) CN Ghosh

The Craft of Intelligence by Allen W Dulles

Fulcrum of Evil: ISI-CIA-Al Qaeda Nexus by MK Dhar (Former Joint Chief of IB)

The Conspirators: Fiction of Facts (A Book on Pakistan's Intelligence) by Brig Yash Mohan, VSM

Silent Warfare: Understanding the World of Intelligence by Abram N Shulsky & Gary J Schmitt

Wages of Crime: Black Markets, Illegal Finance and the Underworld Economy by R T Naylor

The Peace Keepers: Indian Police Service (IPS) by SR Arun, IPS

Para-Military Forces: Central Reserve and Foreign Policy by Dr AK Pasha

Human Rights Training by Dr S Subramanian, IPS

Industrial Espionage: Causes and Cure by Dr S Subramaniam, IPS

Executive Protection by Dr S Subramaniam, IPS

CIA's Eye on South Asia by Anuj Dhar, Journalist

Threat to Security: How Secured is India from within by PC Dogra, IPS (Former DGP, Punjab)

Effective Interrogation: Naxalism, Police, Intelligence by G Chatterjee (Former Intelligence Officer)

Financial Terrorism: Black Money and the Indian Elite by BR Lall, IPS (Former: Joint Director, CBI)

White Collar Crimes X-Posed by Thakur Shailendra Nath